Facts

Other Books by the same author

Life in the World Unseen
More about Life in the World Unseen
Here and Hereafter (originally 'The ABC of Life')
Heaven and Earth
More Light

Facts

~ more spirit communications
from
Monsignor Robert Hugh Benson

Received & Recorded by

Anthony Borgia

© Tony Ortzen

All rights reserved. No portion of this book may be reproduced or utilised in any form or by any means, electronic or mechanical, including photocopying, recording or retrieval system, without the prior permission in writing of the publisher. Nor it is to be otherwise circulated in any form or binding or cover other than that in which it is published.

First published 1946
This edition 2020

Published by
Saturday Night Press Publications
England

snppbooks@gmail.com
www.snppbooks.com

ISBN 978-1-908421-40-1

Cover design: *Ann Harrison (SNPP) with permission to use a painting of Venice by Marjorie Hesford.*

Contents

		Page
	Preface	7
1.	Introductory	9
2.	They That Mourn	26
3.	Justice and Mercy	43
4.	Prayer	60
5.	The Lord's Prayer	74
6.	Prayer Answered	96
7.	Baptism	108
8.	Vicarious Atonement	123
9.	'Thy Kingdom Come'	135

Preface

The spirit communicator of this book has, in previous volumes, dealt solely with descriptions of the spirit world and life in spirit lands generally, and he has hitherto touched only incidentally upon matters concerning 'faith and morals'.

In the present work, he abandons descriptions of spirit life, and instead shows the attitude of the spirit world towards certain theological beliefs with reference to a number of texts from the New Testament.

A common experience which so many of us undergo when we pass to the spirit world is that of the necessity of readjusting, in varying degrees, our views upon many things in the light of newly gained knowledge and altered position. Our very mode of living undergoes a drastic change.

If the laity find this need for the readjustment of views after 'death', how much more so must it be the case in one who was a priest of the Church, and who on earth was compelled (at least outwardly) to regard all communications from the spirit world as 'dealings with the devil'!

My friendship with the communicator of this book, who was a distinguished priest in earth life, began in 1909 (five years before he went to the spirit world) in circumstances of so pleasant a nature that we are both unlikely ever to forget them. His passing has not meant the severance of that friendship, but its intensification, and that has been accomplished in the one way possible—by direct communication with him.

In fact, since he took up his residence in the spirit world, I have had many more opportunities of meeting him, together with a goodly company of mutual friends, than would ever have been possible had he remained here upon earth. It has been my happy experience to act as his earthly amanuensis throughout the previous scripts, and in this latest instance to record some of the details 'of his 'revised theology'.

Anthony Borgia

Introductory

In speaking to my friends of earth once again, there is one preliminary observation that I would like to make. It is this: the spirit world is a vast place, and the activities of its inhabitants are upon a gigantic scale.

That part of the spirit world in which it is my great good fortune to live represents but an infinitesimal part of the whole, but to attempt to describe every feature of that part at any one time and within the covers of a single volume would be impossible. The problem is a common one that confronts every person who wishes to return to earth, when the opportunity presents itself, to recount his experiences of the spirit world. When the theme has been chosen, what shall be set down; what shall be omitted?

Such being the case, some of my good friends of earth are bound, in some measure, to be disappointed because I have not dealt fully enough with some point which has aroused their interest. That I very much regret, and I hope that these few preliminary words will help to make the position clear.

In the matter of the theme of these writings I have not, at any time, relied upon my own judgement, but I have been fortunate in always having at my side wise and gifted counsellors, whose experiences of life in the spirit world and of the varying conditions of communication with the earth world, are wide. These friends are constantly giving me the benefit of their sterling advice upon all matters relative to these writings, and I have in all cases followed their advice.

Hitherto we have confined our descriptions and discussions to the spirit world and the life which some of us, its inhabitants, live in these beautiful realms.

Some people on earth profess to take little or no interest in the kind of life which is led by a great community of us in spirit lands. They prefer, they would assert, something a little less 'material', a little more elevated than descriptions of delightful houses and gardens, of beautiful landscapes, of pleasant occupations and enjoyable recreations. They feel that such things do not accord with what should be their ultimate destiny in the 'life hereafter'. But I would ask such folk to devote a few quiet moments to the subject, and to ask themselves just what they feel the 'life hereafter' really ought to be, if they had the ordering of such things.

Wherein would they find their happiness? Of what nature would they wish their surroundings to be? One cannot imagine such folk being contented to spend aeons of time in the spirit world occupied in some form of spirit contemplation to the exclusion of all other forms of activity—if contemplation can, in this sense, be considered an activity at all.

My experience has been that people who call the loudest for a highly spiritualised form of life in the spirit world are the first, when they come here to the spirit world, to be profoundly glad to see about them the many examples of *material* beauty and grandeur taking an outward form that they can quickly and easily recognise and understand.

Indeed, the multiplicity of delights that are to be encountered has the effect of speedily and effectively driving out of their heads any ideas of spending valuable time in contemplation—except to contemplate upon their great good fortune in finding things as they are, and not as they might have been inclined to advocate when they were incarnate. So many things are nicer in the abstract than in the concrete: a lifetime spent in contemplation might be one of them.

I have been advised that the time would be appropriate for me to leave for the present, at least, any further account of our life in these realms and, instead, to treat of other matters of equal importance concerning our two worlds, yours and mine. But before doing so, there are one or two considerations which I should like to place before you since they have a direct bearing upon our principal theme.

You must know, then, that the spirit world has been in existence for countless millions of years of earthly time. The earth world is but a toddling infant by comparison with the seemingly incalculable age of the spirit world. Coeval with the age of the spirit world are the laws that govern it.

These laws have remained constant, unvarying, invariable, and in absolute continuity of existence and operation throughout this colossal period of time.

The spirit world, with great hosts of its inhabitants, has seen the dawn of the earth world, and those same great hosts have watched, too, the formation of the spirit spheres that are situated, as I have elsewhere explained to you, in concentric circles around the earth. It is not my purpose to discuss the formation of the spirit spheres since it has no direct reference to our present subject.

Beings in the exalted realms have beheld the evolution of man on earth, and they have assisted in that evolution. They have watched man's steady spiritual and material progression.

Man, as he now is, was not created upon the instant, as the Church teaches, in the image and likeness of his Creator. He was slowly and steadily evolved from a lower order of creatures. The image and likeness were to come later. The Paradise of Eden is the best attempt at an explanation of the 'creation' of man that man himself could *at that time* evoke. The story of the first man and woman, whom the earth world has come to name Adam and Eve, is a natural corollary to the legend of their creation.

Had the story ended with this supposed couple enjoying to the end of their earthly days the pleasures and delights of their ideal abode, the earth world would have been saved an immensity of pain and suffering, of persecution, wars, and bloodshed, and a score of other tribulations and calamities. But some explanation was bound to be given as to why this earthly paradise was not still flourishing. And so there was invented the utterly nonsensical and completely false doctrine of the Fall of Man, and that from this fall the whole of mankind is for ever tainted with 'original sin'.

The various Churches of the earth-plane are by no means of one mind upon what is exactly meant by original sin. But the different interpretations of the doctrine have one point in common—*they are all equally and completely erroneous!*

It is the belief of the Church to which I belonged when I was on earth that Adam and Eve were immortal in their earthly bodies, that the process known as physical death was as yet unknown. These two individuals, therefore, were so constituted that they were living, as it were, in two worlds at once. They were, in fact, partly of the spirit world and partly of the earth world.

It was the sin of these supposed first parents that led

the Father of the universe to invent the 'death' of the physical body. He cast them out of Paradise, condemned them to 'death', and that 'death' became communicable, like some pestilent disease, to all future generations of mankind. The whole fabrication of the history of the creation of man and his subsequent disaster is a gross insult to the Infinite Mind.

The complexity of Church doctrines and creeds that have their origin or basis in the fable of our first parents is a totally inadequate attempt to explain what the early churchmen were completely unable to explain.

The Christian civilisation of the earth world dates the commencement of its history at about two thousand years ago of earthly time. Two thousand years: they are but a grain of sand, one single grain of sand, in a whole vast desert of time. What was happening on earth before those two thousand years commenced?

The earth, you are taught to believe, was mostly in a state of paganism, where the people worshipped a multiplicity of gods, and changed their gods as their fancy led them. The great Father had, in fact, more or less abandoned his earthly children for countless millions of years, and He only, at last, bethought Him to send 'salvation' to earth two thousand years ago, after aeons and aeons of time had passed by in neglect. Such, in effect, is what you are asked to believe, as we, of the spirit world, see it.

The devil, of course, appears in this story of the first man and woman. It is he who caused their downfall. One might ask: who is this mysterious devil who, ever since his first great achievement in the Garden of Eden, has spent his time and energies 'wandering through the world for the ruin of souls'?

On a former occasion I spoke to you about this seemingly ever-present gentleman. After hearing so much about him when I was incarnate, one of the early questions that I asked concerned the existence—or otherwise—of Satan. Did such a person really exist? I was told that there was no truth whatever in the story that somewhere in the lowest realms there was a Prince of Evil whose sole object was to place himself in direct opposition to the Father of all good, and whose function was to lure souls into the commission of base deeds that would encompass their eternal damnation.

That, I was assured, was all sheer nonsense. If one were to traverse the dark realms and make a really comprehensive survey of those regions, one might, after careful elimination, find one or more souls who were considerably lower in the scale of evil than their fellows. Conceivably, one might even find one who was so debased that those in evil might feel inclined to regard him as something of a leader in evil ways.

That there is one who is indisputably the Prince of Evil—no, he simply does not exist. Every inch of the dark realms has been surveyed by beings of the highest realms, and they have so far failed to discover this personage. Not that they set out for that purpose! The knowledge that all such high beings possess tells them that there is no such person as the devil. But in the sense that all evil people in the realms of darkness can be called devils, then there are many devils.

The devil is supposed to take upon himself many disguises. In the story of the Garden of Eden he became a serpent. At the present day upon earth, the Church claims that the devil manifests himself by masquerading as an 'angel of light' in the 'seance chamber', where he efficiently carries on his fell work of luring souls to their doom. In such cases, then, the devil has even, on occasion, claimed to have been a former priest of the Church!

We can afford to smile at such stupidity, but we are also saddened by it. Living in the spirit world, as I do, with all the beauties and marvels, all the joys and delights, and the heaven-sent opportunities of doing good and useful work ever around us, we can see the profound darkness of so much of what we called religious thought when we lived on the earth-plane. We can recall how strenuously we upheld some doctrine or another as being vitally important to the soul's 'salvation', only to find, when we came to live for all time in the spirit world, that such doctrine counts for nothing, literally nothing. It shows itself for what it is—completely meaningless.

It becomes disintegrated by the great truths that are before us here. Such, for example, is soon to be discovered in the story of our supposed first parents and the doctrine of original sin. It is as impossible to find Adam and Eve, or their equivalent, in the spirit world, as it is impossible to find the devil, and for the same reason. They simply do not exist. It might be possible to ascertain who were among the first of the earth world's inhabitants to show the first signs of dawning intelligence, but who would be the better for the discovery?

The whole great organisation of the earth world has been a slow process of evolution and progression. Man did not suddenly come into being at the word of the Father of the universe, as it were, overnight. The whole procedure has occupied thousands of years of earthly time, and it is still going on, despite appearances to the contrary! The earth world and its inhabitants, whether man or beast, are corruptible.

But the etheric counterpart of the earth world—for such we might roughly designate the spirit spheres that are concentric with it—and the spiritual element of both man and beast, all these are incorruptible. Primitive man upon the earth-plane was subject to the very same natural laws as are you at this moment of time. From the instant of its beginning, the earth world has been subject to the laws of corruption. Primitive man 'died', undergoing therein a process exactly similar to that which I underwent, though the circumstances of it might be widely different. That same primitive man is now resident in the spirit world.

His features have changed throughout the countless years until he has grown like ourselves in general conformation. He has progressed by virtue of his birth-right, the same birth-right that we all possess, you, who are incarnate, and I, who am discarnate, together with all the innumerable millions of souls in both worlds. And that birth-right is the full and free title to, and the ability and opportunity for, limitless progression. Who is to say how far progression can be extended in each individual? To us here it seems limitless.

Primitive man, as the very early inhabitants of earth are called, is here with us in the spirit world. Such souls are the occupants of the highest spheres. They came here as they left the earth world—you would regard them as savages. Their features would perhaps suggest that appellation to you.

To the dwellers of the spirit world of those far-off times they were human souls, rough cast, maybe, lacking in knowledge of spiritual things such as you enjoy today, but nevertheless possessed of some glimmerings of spiritual light. With their advent into the spirit world, they were soon taken in hand by wondrous souls who had never had an incarnate existence, but who belonged to the world of spirit, and to the world of spirit alone. Under such magnificent instruction and guidance, these primitive souls have progressed out of all recognition of their former selves.

At this moment of time you would be unable to identify a being who was once called 'primitive man' nor differentiate him from any other inhabitant from his own high realm. While primitive man was being carefully evolved into a higher being in the spirit world, his brother still upon earth was undergoing a similar transformation until he bore all the characteristics which are familiar to mankind at this present moment.

The spiritual and material evolution of man upon the earth-plane is still going on, and it will ever so continue. What is to be the great end is not for me to hazard a guess.

Such things are the closely guarded secrets of the highest spheres, and it is problematical whether we should be the better off if we were to be fully informed upon the matter.

Religiously speaking, man has divided his earthly existence so far into two epochs—Christian and pre-Christian. In the latter epoch, you are told, the world was spiritually dark. Mankind was still labouring as best he could under the supposed wrath of God for the commission of the great 'sin' of our first parents.

According to the ancient books and chronicles, a 'deliverer' would be sent, but of the time and place and circumstances of his coming no man knew. At length, at a period which is reckoned at about two thousand years ago, a great being was born upon earth. By some he was hailed as the long-awaited deliverer; by others this was rigorously denied. After nearly two thousand years have passed, there still remains the same divided thought as to whether or not God sent His deliverer.

The birth upon the earth-plane of that illustrious soul so many years ago was eventually to stir men's minds as they had not been stirred before. Manuscripts were made supposedly containing the many acts and words performed and spoken during his short life on earth, together with his teachings. From this, there has been built up a vast theology, so abstruse, so complex, so incomprehensible, that no man can explain it, and so controversial that scores of distinct and separate and opposed religious sects have arisen upon the earth-plane, each claiming to be more or less the only true means of the soul's 'salvation'.

As a priest of one of the principal of these religious denominations, I upheld, when I was upon earth, all its doctrines and creeds. When I eventually came to live in the spirit world, I found that the whole of my theological 'knowledge' was completely negatived or stultified by my first sight of the truths of the spirit world, of its people, and of its laws. I found that as far as the people of earth were concerned, they had never lived for one single fraction of a moment under the wrath of God, for the all-sufficing reason that the Great Father of Heaven cannot entertain wrath against any person or persons whatsoever for any reason or reasons whatsoever.

How do I know this, it may be asked? The answer is simple: *it is common knowledge in the spirit world.* We, in these realms, all know it. Therein lies the immeasurable beauty of it. It is apparent at every turn. The 'wrath of God' is a stupid and wicked fiction. Numberless false theories have been propounded from it, and numberless false doctrines have been formulated. The most elementary acquaintance with the laws of the spirit world will at once show that the 'wrath of God' is a contradiction of terms. The two words cannot exist together. That is also common knowledge in these realms, elementary knowledge. The wrath of God, indeed!

But that is not all. Jesus, the great teacher who was born upon earth two thousand years ago, was cast out of the earth world violently and shamefully by the people of earth. This tragic transition was an act of expiation to the Eternal Father for the wrath He felt and as a means of saving the earth world's inhabitants. So it is still taught in the churches of earth. A blood sacrifice of His only son!

Such beliefs as these are primitive and barbaric, and monstrous when viewed in the light of the great truths of the spirit world as we know and understand them here.

Since the first moment when the earth world existed, exalted beings of the highest realms have had it in their charge. As you contemplate the chaotic conditions prevailing at the present time, you may be disposed to think that these same beings have dismally failed in their task. That is not so. They have not failed.

When man was first evolved from a lower order of creatures, he was constantly watched and aided. As primitive man grew in intelligence, he was in active communication with the spirit world by the operations of those higher senses which are inherent in every soul, but which lie fallow and undeveloped chiefly through man's ignorance.

The progression of the earth world and its inhabitants has been slow, steady, and uninterrupted throughout the thousands upon thousands of years of its life.

Never for one instant of time were the two worlds out of direct contact. All this while, man was—and still—is exercising his free will. Sometimes he listened to the voices from the spirit world—then all was well. Many times his ears were deaf to those voices—then all was ill. The guidance was ever there. The 'road of salvation' was always the same. To teach that one great soul should suffer all the torments of persecution and a horrible 'death' in order to save the world from 'damnation', and to teach that this same tragedy should be demanded by the Father of Heaven to appease His wrath, is not only revolting in itself to us here in the spirit world, but it is far, far worse than that. It is the grossest libel, the greatest defamation—to put it at its very least—that could ever be contemplated upon the character and nature and the very essence of the Great Father of the universe.

We who live in the spirit world can see the might and majesty of the Father's great creation—the universe. But we can also see what is far greater and far more majestic—man himself. It will be said, perhaps, that there cannot be anything very mighty and majestic about those hideous denizens of the dark realms I have described. No! In their present state most certainly not.

But resident within every one of those unfortunate beings there is the germ of spiritual evolution and progression, and therein lies his might and majesty. Remember those 'primitive' men who have so evolved and spiritually progressed that they are now dwellers in the highest realms, who are possessed of immense knowledge and wisdom, and who are, in every sense, wondrous souls.

Throughout the whole course of the earth world's existence, there have been born into it great teachers of great truths. There has been a long succession of them in the past, and they will so continue to come in the future. It rests with man himself whether he heeds such teachers—or rejects them.

Entrance to the spirit world is gained in one way only-through the 'death' of the physical body. No person or persons can assign to a single soul any other place in the spirit world than that which that soul has merited for himself. He cannot be saved through the intermediation of another, whoever that other may be. His merits for a realm of beauty as his residence must be his own merits. No other person can share his burden if his life upon earth has been hideous. He pays the penalty himself, as I have already tried to indicate to you.

If this be the case—and it is—of what use is the constant repetition of elaborate creeds and the perpetual reiteration from dismal and protracted formularies, in both of which the spiritual life of incarnate man is hemmed in and suffocated? There is no magic formula upon the pronouncing of which a safe journey to the spirit world is assured and a salubrious destination procured. Our merits alone will provide those, and no one can plead for us before the Great Throne. Our life upon earth is our sole advocate and our most eloquent—for the state of our being when we arrive in the world of spirit. And that same life is also our incorruptible judge.

The many orthodox religions that have sprung up during the course of the two thousand years past are all of them completely out of touch with the realities of the spirit world. They are all of them based upon entirely false values and conceptions.

Some religious bodies are presumptuous enough to profess to *know* exactly what is in the Heavenly Father's mind. Others lay stress upon the 'saving power' of Jesus, that great soul whom the earth rejected two millenniums ago. They claim that none can be 'saved' except they be 'saved' through him. By constantly reiterating this in the many rather fulsome and frigid prayers that are said publicly. It seems to be believed that some magical process will be put into operation whereby the soul can be assured that wherever else it may go when 'death' takes place. It will not go for all eternity to hell.

Indeed, it may be said that Orthodoxy bases its only hope of the soul's 'salvation' upon the merits of another. It is in this respect that Orthodoxy has taken the spirit world and made of it a Christian spirit world, or, at least, the religious teachers would say that the Christian element more than predominates.

As an inhabitant of the spirit world, I soon discovered that the spirit world is so much greater than what the earth world denominates 'the Christian religion'. Indeed, it is way beyond all earthly religions of whatever denomination. It is made up of peoples from every quarter of the earth world, representing every school of earthly religious thought.

In the realms wherein I dwell, we have cast aside for ever the allegiance to the Church of our earthly lives. We have no orthodox religion here. We are all of one mind, and that mind is regulated by the strict truth.

I have already recounted to you how in certain quarters of these realms one can find churches, such as are to be found upon the earth-plane, supported by adherents of a variety of religious sects. But that makes no difference whatever to my statement that we have done with earthly religions. These churches are permitted to exist under conditions that are perfectly understood and as perfectly defined. They merely form a carefully segregated community that is bound by strict rules. There is no harm in erecting a beautiful edifice in the style and manner of earthly ecclesiastical buildings. It is what takes place within them that is subject to the most exact laws.

The spirit world, in short, is undenominational. Orthodoxy may make as many claims as it wishes in respect of its self-arrogated right to be the guardian of man's 'immortal soul'. Admittance to the spirit world is not through any one Church or collection of Churches; nor is it obtained through the merits of any one person or body of persons.

There is no saint of the ecclesiastical calendar whose merits will assist us to escape or dodge the results of our wrong-doing when we were incarnate. We must pay ourselves alone. Nor will membership to the Church which makes the greatest claims of assuring 'salvation' for ourselves avail us one fraction. We undergo the experience of passing through the portal of physical death alone, although we may have willing help in the actual procedure from those who are already discarnate. But it stops there.

Such helpers cannot assign us to any destination other than that which we have earned for ourselves. It is plain, therefore, as the noonday sun—and I speak from exact experience—that the tragedy that took place at Calvary nigh upon two thousand years ago, although a personal sacrifice of sublime beauty, yet that tragedy does not and cannot have any bearing upon the individual souls who have been born upon earth since that time, or who were born at that time or before it.

That great event demonstrated a profound truth of which I and countless millions are the living witnesses, namely, that the death of the physical body is but the beginning of a new life and that as we have sown during our life in the earth world, so shall we reap in the life of the spirit world. But great as that sacrifice was, neither its grandeur nor its merits are communicable, just as the sacrifice and merits of us all are incommunicable. We are each and every one of us responsible for our own misdeeds.

All this, you will perhaps say, is a far cry from the

supposed story of our first parents. It is not so really. Adam and Eve were our first parents, so you are taught. They committed the first 'sin', and were punished by being cast out from their 'garden of paradise'. Up to this time these two individuals were strangely constructed. They were, in fact, immortal in their physical bodies while at the same time they were living upon a corruptible earth. They lost this strange attribute when they committed their 'sin' and 'death' was introduced. The whole race of mankind that was to come was involved in the crash, and it was only the promise of the visitation 'from on high' to the earth-plane of one who would redeem the earth world that made life possible upon it.

I have tried to show you that this story is fantastic, and in doing so to bridge the immense gap between the formation of the world, with its subsequent steady evolution, and that era which commenced two thousand years ago. Adam and Eve as our first parents had no existence in fact. The story is a fantasy. Jesus was born upon earth two thousand years ago, and he is today an immense force upon the earth-plane. That is fact. The fantasy and the fact have no relation whatever to one another, but the Church has made the one dependent and consequent upon the other. From this there have arisen all the strange variety of religious sects and religious observances that are to be seen throughout the earth.

It is against every law of the spirit world that one person can assume responsibility for another's wrongdoing. There are no merits belonging to another person of which we can avail ourselves and by which we can evade our responsibilities. But it will be said, this great soul who perished so tragically, is different. He is one apart. He is Divine. He is the Son of God come down to earth to redeem us. He is, in fact, God Himself.

With God all things are possible. Therefore, by virtue of his Divinity, Jesus can wash away our sins if we have sufficient faith and do what the Church teaches. We must be repentant, of course, but being repentant, we have one who will plead our cause, and by the merits of his supreme sacrifice we shall be saved.

That is a very comforting and comfortable thought and belief, but there is just one flaw. *It simply is not true.*

They That Mourn

It has been remarked of previous writings that I have made no mention whatever of the great soul whom the world knows as Jesus of Nazareth, and that seemingly, as far as I am concerned, he might never have existed.

My abstention from all such mention so far has been deliberate. It was fully intended that such should be the case from the moment that we set down our first word in these accounts of my experiences in the spirit world. But the time has now come when it would be profitable to speak not only of the Nazarene, as he is so often called, but also to discuss the book, or some parts of it at least, in which are chronicled a *few* of the teachings which he gave forth during his short life on earth.

For many hundreds of earthly years, the New Testament has been claimed to be the inspired word of God. Opinions differ upon this one point, but there is still greater diversity of opinion upon much that is contained in the gospels. So wide is the latter divergence that literally hundreds of different Christian religions and religious sects have sprung up all over the earth world, each professing to be a 'true' religion, if not *the* 'true' religion.

Some individuals go still further and claim that absolute belief in the contents of the book is itself sufficient for the 'salvation' of the soul, and that without that belief the soul is lost, condemned for all eternity to remain not only without the gates of heaven, but at a very great distance from them.

One religious denomination in particular proclaims itself to be the sole depository of truth upon earth, with an infallible interpretation of the gospels. How then, do we in the spirit world regard the New Testament? Surely, it might be said, you in the spirit world have the opportunity of ascertaining the truth upon all such matters, especially upon the various texts in the gospels over which so much controversy has arisen, or which are still obscure in their meaning.

Certainly we have the means in the spirit world of getting at the truth in such a case. But suppose we were to give the truth, should we not be charged with giving just another interpretation and so adding to the confusion that already exists?

Should we not also be suspected of trying to found yet another religion upon earth that already contains far, far too many? Finally, why should any 'interpretation' that I might offer to my friends on earth be considered the right interpretation?

It is a risk that is worth taking. In spite, therefore, of what one Church emphatically teaches, namely, that private judgement in such matters is heartily to be condemned, I would ask my friends who have followed my writings thus far to view what I have to say in the light of spiritual truths.

I would ask them to cast from their minds, at least for the moment, but better still *for all time*, such doctrines and creeds as they already possess, and to come with me upon a pleasant journey whereon we will explore some parts and passages of the New Testament.

We will not essay any new interpretation. We will merely take some passages of the gospels and see how they compare with the truth as it exists in the spirit world.

'What is this?' I can hear someone declare, 'Are you suggesting that Jesus of Nazareth did not teach the truth?' Most emphatically I am not suggesting such a thing. He told the absolute truth, but it remained for those who humbly professed to be his followers in after years to do just the opposite.

What has been set down in the four gospels is but a tiny fraction of the great body of teachings that were originally given forth. They have been inaccurately set down; they were not—and are not—the inspired word of God. They have been mistranslated, misinterpreted, suffered interpolations and distortions, and they have been tampered with until it seems more than remarkable if a vestige of the truth can remain.

From this chaos, there have arisen an immense variety of dogmas and ritualistic practices that have no bearing whatever upon the spiritual progression of a single soul. And in the very centre of this distortion stands Jesus of Nazareth, who gave the truth in the first instance, and who, through the operation of that catalogue of accidents which I have just enumerated as befalling the Scriptures, now finds himself elevated into the position of God Himself.

To Jesus, in virtue of his deified position, are attributed the most outrageously impossible functions and attributes. His life on earth is almost one of the major 'mysteries' of the Christian religion because he is God Himself, who has come down to earth to live there as man.

The whole doctrine of the Incarnation is one of the most fantastic inventions of the theologians of past centuries on earth—to take just one instance from many of how the mind of man can build up strange mysteries concerning the spirit world where, in good truth, no mysteries exist.

The laws that govern the spirit world are not complex laws that none can understand. There are many things in spirit life which we cannot understand yet, just as there are many things upon earth which cannot yet be understood.

But just as you have great minds on earth who can and will—eventually solve such mysteries, so in the spirit world are there still greater minds who can—and will provide an answer to our riddles.

At the moment, our state of mental evolution has not sufficiently advanced for us to be capable of understanding were an explanation to be given to us. But with all such matters we can see plainly the *reason* for some law, or truth, or whatever it may be. We are not treated to a farrago of words that collectively possess not one grain of meaning or sense, only to be told that it is a 'mystery', or something that under Divine Providence we are not meant to know.

When we come to discuss the New Testament, we shall find that a great deal of what it contains has *no meaning* whatever when viewed in the light of our knowledge of the spirit world and of spirit life in general. We are not here concerned with what may have been set down in the original documents, as to whether we are considering a mistranslation. A reference to originals will get us no further forward.

In setting down these records, the writers of them simply filled in any hiatus that might have occurred in their work by thoughts and ideas entirely their own. Some of these interpolations—indeed, a great many of them—are claimed as the sayings of Jesus. Now, in the spirit world we know positively whether any particular dictum—provided that it makes sense—can be of the authorship of Jesus because we know that he was himself under such supremely careful guardianship from the spirit world that no errors would have been permitted to him in the delivering of his spiritual teachings.

The untruth is not of Jesus, but of his chroniclers and subsequent transcribers. It happens, then, that when we try to give some clear meaning to what obviously sounds preposterous as it stands, we find that the sense of the original has been so altered in many cases that words, in their ordinary, everyday use, have almost ceased to have any meaning. Theologians have become adept in twisting words beyond all recognition of their true import. With the adoption of such practices, there is no limit to the number of meanings or interpretations that can be accorded to any simple sentence of words.

An impediment would seem to arise from the belief that the Scriptures are the inspired word of God. Therefore, it follows that however much we should feel that a certain text is wrong as it stands if we take the words in their rational meaning, there must be a correct interpretation if one could only discover what it was. This the theologians have brazenly and presumptuously done. I say 'presumptuously' because in so many instances they profess to know and declaim the precise 'will of God'.

What causes perhaps the widest departure from the truth is the work of interpolators that has been carried out through the whole length of the four gospels. When those of us who have some acquaintance with the gospels arrive in the spirit world, we can see so much that is in *complete and total contradiction* to so much that was rigorously upheld by us when we were incarnate. This revelation may be a shock to some of us. It is a shock, however, that we can soon overcome! A knowledge of spiritual truths and the experience of the life we live here in these realms are sufficient at once to demonstrate clearly what is a precise statement of incontrovertible fact appearing in the gospels and what is pure fiction.

The misadventures which the Scriptures have suffered at the hands of the recorders, transcribers and translators have given rise to the large company of theologians who have strenuously endeavoured to make spiritual sense of what is utterly meaningless. Controversies have occurred where in some cases acute minds have perceived the truth, proclaimed it, have been branded as heretics by their brothers in religion, have been condemned, and finally have been ceremoniously deprived of their earthly lives.

Such a vast structure of mystery and obscuration has been built around the Scriptures in the fantastic interpretation of them as to provide the earth world with scores of ritualistic practices and ceremonies as well as obscure creeds and dogmas, all of which, the earth is taught, are collectively or individually necessary for the 'salvation' of the soul.

Instead of making the spirit world and its laws, and the process of getting into it, a matter of plain, sensible fact, to be understood in the same sensible way in which you understand your ordinary functions on earth, the spiritual teachers of earth have circumscribed the whole subject with such enigmas and involutions that religion has become, as it were, a separate part of life on earth.

The very act of 'dying' is the operation of a simple, natural law. By its operation, man casts off his physical body, which has served him for his life on earth. He then finds himself in the spirit world, there to be resident for all time. It is the normal, natural outcome of his earthly life. It is inescapable for all persons without exception, of high degree or low. It was never intended, under the dispensation that has provided the whole scheme of life on the earth-plane and in the spirit world, that the spirit world should be regarded by the incarnate as some fearful and frightening unknown destination for which all on earth are bound, and from which no one has ever returned, or ever will return, to recount what has befallen him after he has left the earth world.

The spirit world has been wrapped in a deadly silence, therefore, a silence which must forever remain unbroken. It is small wonder that so many of the dwellers of earth are terrified at the prospect of leaving it at their dissolution. In the meantime, to try to alleviate this fear, the Churches give voice to inexplicable utterances exhorting their followers to have 'faith', and to cast themselves upon the mercy of God. And the great book that should have been such a treasure of facts concerning life in both our worlds, yours and mine, has been so mishandled by those who have claimed to be its custodians as to offer very little light upon matters that are so important to all people.

What we have just set down are one or two observations which I thought it expedient to make before we undertake to consider some passages from the New Testament.

To these remarks I would add that we shall not pursue a direct course, so to speak, but rather consider such passages as deal with a particular feature of spirit life or with spirit truths in general.

Once again, I would say that we are not here concerned with what may or may not appear in the original documents or in others of an early date, but only what appears in the printed books of this present moment of your time. Whatever theologians may know of the original is of little or no concern to the ordinary man. He wants plain facts in such a case, facts that are readily accessible, and, moreover, facts that are stated in terms that he can easily understand, not in words which state one thing but which, by the tortuous ways of theologians, are made to signify exactly the opposite.

In the chapter in which is set down the famous Sermon on the Mount, we find the sermon opens with a series of statements, each prefixed by the word *blessed*, and which are known as the beatitudes. Let us together examine one of them: *Blessed are they that mourn, for they shall be comforted.* How? Wherein lies the blessing?

Incalculable millions of people on earth have undergone the crushing experience of bereavement. To those who have experienced it, it can be crushing. The loved one is gone; the voice that was so well known is silent, and seemingly silent forever. Nothing can fill the desolate blank that is caused by the departure for an unknown destination of that cherished soul. *That* is a doubtful blessing, to say the least, which requires such sorrow and sadness to call it down upon one. Or is it that the comfort is so sublime, so soothing to the troubled mind. a spiritual experience of such beauty, that it is well worth our while to lose some dear friend or relation merely to experience it? That would seem too nonsensical to be worthy of a moment's serious thought.

Again we could ask: wherein lies the comfort? The comfort offered by 'faith' in some religious system, perhaps?

It is customary in some cases, where the mourners are of a simple turn of mind, for them to say that it is God's will, and that He has *taken* their lost one. But yet they cannot understand why God should *take* him; for what purpose, especially if accident or illness has cut short the earthly life in its earlier years? So that the average person confronted with bereavement would like to perceive just where is the blessing in his mourning. and whence comes the comfort, for, he will tell you earnestly from the depths of his deep sorrow, he can perceive neither the blessing nor the comfort—and it is comfort he so urgently needs at that moment of desolation.

The theologian will find a great deal in those simple *words, blessed are they that mourn, for they shall be comforted,* but they will be mostly empty words for he cannot answer the questions put to him as to whence the blessing and the comfort.

I can speak from my own experience when upon earth. When I was in the presence of some soul distraught with bereavement, the words of comfort I could give were few and seemed hollow. Indeed, what was there, out of a great fund of theological knowledge, so-called, that I could offer to a soul in such distress? What real fact could I present?

That sufferer in sadness wanted to know so much that I was powerless to answer from the Church's 'teachings'. The best I could do on innumerable occasions was to try to strengthen the friend in his 'faith'; to offer the hope that his prayers, coupled with the powerful intercession of the Church, would be bound to avail, and that the departed soul would be ultimately released from the pains of purgatory—and so on, with a deal more upon the same empty barren lines.

Always was there a feeling of the silence of the tomb. But it was—and is—a silence that is imposed by people on earth who regard the very thought of death of the physical body as morbid. To say from the pulpit or the sanctuary *blessed are they that mourn, for they shall be comforted* to a congregation that includes just one mourner who is in dire need of comfort but cannot obtain it, is to give a public demonstration that there is something fundamentally wrong somewhere.

It has been suggested by a theologian of the Church that the person who is here blessed is he who 'mourns' for his 'sins'. Could there ever be a greater travesty, a wilder distortion, a worse corruption of such *a plain statement of fact* as that the mourner shall be comforted?

Here at the very outset of one of the foremost books upon earth, in the very opening chapters, is the clue, one might almost say, to the whole work. What of death? It is nothing. But thousands upon thousands of people upon earth will at some time or another mourn the loss of their friends or family, and thus will the distress of sorrow be cast upon many who can find no reason, who can see no good purpose why such sorrow—and such crushing sorrow—as that of the mourner should ever come to pass.

Many an overwrought soul has asked, 'Why does God allow it?' They have a poor estimation of what they have been taught to believe is Divine Providence. The providence in this case is hopelessly absent. Even if, as some last hope, they turn to the New Testament, there they will find words which they fail to understand, or understanding their plain meaning, will wonder where they are to find the fulfilment of them. They read that they will be comforted, but merely reading the words and trusting to some elusive spiritual experience to relieve their sorrow is of little or no value in such case. The sorrow's intensity will swamp all other emotions and serve but to aggravate the sorrow by the hopelessness of obtaining relief.

Now, lest my friends should say that I have exaggerated the matter, let me assure them that I have not done so. When I was on earth, there were many occasions, such as will occur with any minister of the Church of whatever denomination, when a sorrowing soul has come for spiritual help and guidance.

The whole body of teachings which Jesus gave in those far-off days was concerned with a two-fold theme: spiritual guidance for people on earth founded upon absolute facts of spirit life and spirit laws: and some account of spirit laws and their operation, with full details of the facts of spirit life.

What is to be read upon the latter subject in the New Testament is but the sorriest fraction of what was originally delivered to his listeners by that great teacher. The larger proportion of those facts were unrecorded. The remainder have been so abridged and distorted, as well as undergoing unauthentic interpolations; they have been so mistranslated and have had cast upon them the wildest and most nonsensical 'interpretations' that the whole book must now be treated with the greatest caution as to what is exact spiritual truth and what is not. The very 'miracles' that were performed by Jesus are demonstrations of the perfect use of psychic faculties under precise and undisputed superintendence of elevated souls from the spirit world.

Even these have been transmogrified into the acts of a divine being, who was in fact God Himself, and to whom, therefore, all things were possible, even to 'raising the dead'.

The whole phrase of *blessed are they that mourn* in its present form is an *isolated* statement of fact. It is, in very truth, but the *text of a whole sermon, as are the remaining 'beatitudes'.* As it stands, it belongs nowhere.

As a theme for a complete discourse, it becomes a title of supreme importance to every soul who is born upon earth, and so it was meant. The meaning is clear to us here in the spirit world. It should have been clear to us when we were on the earth-plane. It would have been clear to us had the full text been set down as it was originally delivered. Even if the bare substance of what was said had been recorded, a splendid result would have been achieved.

Orthodoxy, for hundreds of years, has been ignoring the true meaning of these words, fastening upon them grotesque interpretations to what is a simple statement of truth. Let the theologian search as far and as deeply as he will, he can find no means within the circumscribed orbit of his theology for demonstrating the truth of the assertion that comfort shall be given to the mourner. What can he discover among the Church's creeds and dogmas that will bring that comfort? Faith, or the submission to the will of God? Will either of these afford the slightest comfort? But in place of vague and empty assurances, the truth of spirit laws and their operation *will* bring immense comfort. But the comfort must be sought.

It was never intended that the two worlds, yours and ours, should be treated as two worlds apart, never having, at any time, communication with each other. Why should not our two worlds hold regular and natural converse with each other? That inter-communication *does* exist, has always existed, and, moreover, will always exist. It may have been—and is—carried on by the comparative few, that is true, but that is the loss to the majority.

This intercommunication is one of the true blessings conferred upon both worlds by the Great Mind that has the ordering of such things.

People speak freely and loosely of the will of God because loved ones have gone down into the grave (as they think), and are thenceforth silent. What of the sorrow of those they have left behind them on earth? It is the will of God, then, that such suffering should come upon them. What an infamous imputation it is to the Father of Heaven that He should deliberately plan matters in this universe in such a clumsy way that vast unhappiness should thus be caused throughout the earth!

We, in the spirit world, may know little of the will of God, but at least *we know what He would never do*. He would never cause suffering, of any nature whatsoever, to any single living creature, whether upon your earth or in the spirit world. From the Father of Heaven can come only that which is good and that which is for the happiness of humanity.

Every soul born upon earth must pass through the portal of 'death' before he can take up permanent residence in the spirit world. But with his thus passing to the spirit world with the death of the physical body, the natural and usual circumstances are that others should be left behind to continue their earthly lives until the time comes for them also to pass into these lands. It was not intended that an impregnable barrier of silence should be erected between the people who have passed into the spirit world and the people who are still upon earth.

The means have always existed whereby a natural and normal and happy intercourse between the two worlds should for ever be enjoyed by the inhabitants of both worlds. If people in their dullness and stupidity, or in their blindness and stubbornness, wish to cast aside one of the greatest blessings that a wise dispensation has provided for their comfort, they have no one but themselves to blame for their consequent sorrow. But so many of the great minds of the earth world regard the very thought of direct communication with the two worlds as rubbish, *not proven,* unhealthy, morbid, and even plain madness—according to their great wisdom.

The orthodox Churches uphold them in any objection which they may bring forward. So long as it is an objection, it will be sustained. At the same time, they will uphold the New Testament, every word of it, even that the mourner shall be comforted, though they have not the faintest notion what the words mean, or understanding, in a vague way, what the words *might* mean, they cannot conceive how the comfort is to be afforded, and they are certainly not in any position to provide it.

When Jesus spoke those words, he was making a declaration of absolute truth, and he then proceeded to develop his theme upon the true facts of spiritual laws. He saw about him in those far away times the same sorrow of bereavement as can be witnessed at this very day of earthly time. Humanity has not changed in that respect. There was—and always will be—sorrow at the departure of a friend or relative for the spirit world just so long as human affections endure. Human affections have their rewards; they also have their sufferings, and none so poignant as at the transition of a loved one.

Jesus observed this natural state of things about him. His teaching upon this particular occasion, among many of a similar description, provided the one satisfactory answer to that particular problem of human suffering and sadness. He was not content with merely making the plain statement that the mourner should be comforted, but he told his listeners *how* the mourner could find his comfort. And the means so readily at hand were not 'faith' or submission to the will of God, but the plain facts of communication between the two worlds and how it could be accomplished.

Who was there better qualified to speak upon such a subject than was Jesus himself? No one, for he practised exactly what he preached. His own psychic faculties had been developed during a long period of years under careful guidance from the spirit world. He was able to tell his hearers that 'death' is not the overwhelming tragedy that the folk on earth have always thought it to be. The earth world was in full possession of innumerable blessings conferred upon it by the operation of natural laws. Those same laws are in existence and in operation today, but they are brought into force not by the exponents of Orthodoxy, as they should be, but by the comparative few who are outside the realms of orthodox beliefs.

The problems that confronted Jesus in presenting his theme in full upon the eternal truth that the mourner shall be comforted were problems which have their counterpart in the earth world at this moment of time. His chief opponent was the Church of his day. The chief weapon in the ecclesiastical armoury of all times and all denominations is the weapon of fear, grounded upon strange mysteries and a total and complete misconception of the character and nature of the Father of the universe. The very Scriptures themselves are made to yield textual confirmation of many of the inexplicable beliefs and religious theories upon which Orthodoxy places so much reliance.

The book that should be giving earthly religious teachers the vital truth concerning one's life upon earth and the nature of things that one can expect after earthly life is ended, that book has been made a battleground for religious contentions, with the consequent founding of hundreds of different religious denominations in disagreement with one another, some of them claiming that Jesus was very God Himself, others denying it. Had these same Scriptures not been grossly tampered with, the full truth would have been there for all to see. But with the truth to be seen by the full light of day, it would have pronounce the doom of Orthodoxy, as it was later to be known.

Where would be the authority of any Church not founded and fashioned upon the truth, when the individual was able to provide for himself and *through his own psychic powers* all that was necessary for his spiritual life on earth, and for his safe conduct into the spirit world unassisted by any obscure beliefs, by any elaborate religious performances, and entirely free from fear?

By the practice of this simple 'religion' of communication with the spirit world, not only would the individual be the recipient of spiritual teachings to the betterment of the position which he would occupy immediately upon his transition, but throughout his life upon earth he would be able to converse easily and constantly with such of his friends and relatives who had passed into spirit lands before him.

There would be no mourning, for the mourner would be truly comforted by the converse which he would be able to enjoy at all times with those who had predeceased him. His friends in the spirit world would be able to tell him just how they were faring, just what had befallen them after the experience of 'dying', even as I have been able to tell you, my good friend, of some of my experiences since I came to dwell in these lands.

Did you not regret my passing? I know that you did, but I also know with what joy you welcomed, in those early years, the news that I was well, and I was keenly sensitive of the still greater joy with which you welcomed my return to speak to you. Is there any other way in which this bright and happy state of affairs could have been accomplished? None whatever.

Jesus told those simple folk who sat before him exactly how the mourner could be comforted, and today we are putting into operation the self-same laws whose operation he expounded to them. Jesus had his own friends in the spirit world with whom he constantly spoke, even as is being done upon the earth-plane this day. He could compare the forms of orthodox religion that were about him with the grand truth such as he knew it to be. And he set about bringing the 'glad tidings' before his own folk.

He used words and employed terms that his hearers would unfailingly understand. Occasionally, he veiled his meaning somewhat for reasons of policy, but in no case, during the whole of one particular discourse, did he leave his audience entirely in doubt as to what was his precise meaning. He spoke as any normal person would speak who has knowledge of the facts, and he always had in mind the degree of mentality possessed by his hearers. They were simple people, unlettered and homely, who would be more familiar with homely things than with abstruse teachings upon matters which were far and away beyond their limited comprehension.

The greatest and the simplest teachings of all have not been recorded in the gospels. The doctors of the Church have wrought havoc with what has been set down, and a wide variety of 'interpretations' has been given to a mutilated text. But in spite of them, the mourner will continue to be comforted in the only way possible.

Justice and Mercy

There would seem to be no end to the ingenious interpretations which have been placed upon some of the simplest statements that Jesus made during his short life upon earth. In so many instances, these interpretations are based upon false premises.

So much religiosity has been woven into almost every word that appears in the gospels that the truth of a really plain declaration has been lost in the portentous pronouncements of the theologians and doctors of the Church.

Perhaps it will be argued in the case of the beatitudes, that if, as I assert, they are but the texts of full length discourses, then the theologians have done the best they can with such meagre material at their disposal. They cannot be expected to know the contents of the full discourse. And they would have no right to assume that such and such was said when there is no evidence whatever that it was said. That would be too dangerous a practice, and should be condemned at once.

We, of the spirit world, can see how authority has proceeded in its interpretations. The false premises, to which I have just alluded, are the assumption that the gospels are the inspired word of God, and that Jesus is Himself God.

The gospels have become the principal foundation for most of the religions of the earth world. Religion has become as a separate part of the life of man upon earth, to be practised or to be ignored, as the predilections of the individual may decide. Religion, to so many of the incarnate, means a succession of church-going at regular intervals, or merely a blind belief in every word that is contained in the New Testament, whether it be understood or not.

If one particular religion prefers to introduce a little ritual into its services, that ritual is branded as superstitious by others of an opposing sect. But the truth, as we can see it in the spirit world, is that most religion, as it is at present constituted upon the earth-plane, is itself nothing but sheer superstition. It is superstition begotten of ignorance or lack of knowledge of the truths of life as it is lived in the spirit world.

The afterlife is regarded by the unenlightened as some holy place when, on the one hand, it concerns heaven; of 'hell', it is not pleasant to think. But the Church keeps the prospect of it always before the minds of the 'faithful' as an instrument of fear, to frighten people into a proper way of living while they are upon earth.

Heaven, then, in the minds of so many church-goers is a religious place where the soul will be everlastingly 'caught up' in an ecstasy of pious fervour, where constant 'prayer and praise' will be the order of the day for all eternity—and a great deal more upon the same devout lines. If we behave ourselves while we are upon earth and do the best we can, then, when our time comes, frightful though it may be, we can always throw ourselves upon the mercy of God. *Blessed are the merciful for they shall obtain mercy.*

The interpretation of that is perfectly simple, the churchman will say. It simply means that according as we give mercy to others upon earth, so shall we receive mercy on earth, and so, also, will God be merciful to us.

Then we read that *Blessed are they that hunger and thirst after justice, for they shall have their fill.*

Some renderings of this beatitude prefer the word *righteousness* to *justice*. The righteousness in this case is that of the person who seeks to acquire that spiritual attainment known as piety, a word which we do not like in the spirit world. It savours too much of sanctimoniousness, of the belief that mere piety will bring untold happiness in the spirit world to those who practise it on the earth-plane. It reminds some of us in the spirit world of the many abominations that have taken place in the name of 'religion'.

In the spirit world, piety does not need naming. If by piety is meant *reverencing* God, then we reverence the Father of the universe without the necessity of being cajoled into it or threatened with dire penalties if we do not cultivate it. We do so without being told that it is His due, His right, and that He demands it. The very thought that a person should wish to acquire great piety when upon earth is not a true thought. Few people, *if they are really honest with themselves*, are filled with piety nor do they wish to be so.

With us in the spirit world, God is not some dread Being who must be constantly appeased, propitiated, and dreaded because of the fearful punishments with which He can inflict us upon the instant. We know that to be a completely fantastic conception of the Greatest Being, whose desire is the *happiness* of all living creatures. God is regarded upon earth as the Great Dread Judge of all mankind, but a Judge who is merciful withal, if we merit mercy and ask Him for it.

But if mercy were thus being dispensed of what value would be the justice? Justice, strict justice—and that is the only justice there is in the spirit world—and mercy cannot go together in these lands. Mercy belongs to the earth-plane, not to the spirit world. In what form, or under what conditions, or in what circumstances, could we in the spirit world accord mercy to anyone? There is no form; no conditions or circumstances prevail.

Mercy implies the remission of some penalty or part of a penalty that has been incurred by the commission of an offence. If some person has committed an offence against us, the person who committed it has himself to blame for the consequences. We can forgive sincerely, but the penalty still remains. It is a penalty which the individual has inflicted upon himself. God has not done so. It is not an offence against God.

No person on earth or in the spirit world can offend the Supreme Being. No base thought or idea, no act, however evil or barbarous, no vice, no obscenity, no blasphemies or maledictions, can come within a thousand thousand miles of the Father of the universe. Any one of the catalogue of spiritual horrors which I have just enumerated can—and will—woefully injure a fellow mortal, but most of all they will injure the perpetrators. They have not offended God; they have brought dire disaster upon themselves. They have broken the laws of the spirit world, among the chief of which is the law of cause and effect. Would the Father of Heaven mitigate one iota of the punishment due to breaking of one of the natural laws? If He were to do so, where would strict justice be?

The idea that man is constantly offending God is crude. Allied with it is the similarly crude notion that God inflicts punishments not only upon individuals, but upon whole nations and continents. The wars that man wages upon earth are, so you are told by learned theologians, direct acts inflicted by God in punishment for the evil way of living which has been adopted by a belligerent nation or nations.

Both contestants are included within this condemnation so that we have the spectacle of two or more nations killing each other, depriving each other of their normal span of life on earth, as the considered method of an all-wise and supreme Being of bringing punishment upon erring mankind. What a gross travesty! And when great storms and hurricanes and pestilences sweep through the earth world, leaving disaster and desolation and sorrow behind them, these also are the product of the same infinite Mind. Another gross travesty!

Let me say once more: from the Father of the universe can come nothing which is not of the highest and greatest good. Wars and storms and hurricanes are not the work of God. War is the work of man, and of man only; meteorological upheavals are the work of natural forces only.

The Father of the universe is not an awful Judge 'who shall come to judge the living and the dead.' He judges no one. Whence, then, comes the mercy and upon what account? Where can we in the spirit world show mercy? We cannot judge; we cannot condemn; we cannot sentence. Forgiveness for an offence—yes, we can give that, and we do so with heartfelt sincerity. But with all our forgiveness freely and fully and finally given, we cannot remove one tiny element of the effects that certain causes have brought about in the state of him who has offended us.

We can—and we do—help such an individual as an expression of the fact that we have forgiven and forgotten the fault in our brother to the fullest extent. We can help him to redeem the spiritual ground he has lost. The forgiveness has achieved nothing of itself beyond establishing the right kind of relationship between two people. We may wish with all our hearts that we could ameliorate their unhappy position; we might be filled with mercy towards those who have injured us. That feeling of mercy will translate itself into a deep sympathy and understanding, but that is as far as it proceeds. The self-inflicted penalties remain just the same; we cannot abate them one fraction.

Mercy is a quality which can only be practised upon earth, and we merit a rich reward for our showing that splendid quality during our earthly lives. But as soon as we pass into the spirit world, mercy ceases. Justice takes its place, and justice is the operation of the law of cause and effect. It is a justice which is incorruptible, infallible, impartial, unfailing. There is no evading it; it must exert itself upon all persons alike, of whatever nation, creed, colour, age or sex.

Blessed are they that seek justice, for they shall have their fill. Many seek justice upon earth, and fail to obtain it. Here in the spirit world they receive their fill. The measure is full and brimming over, I do assure you. Those who have denied giving that justice when on earth, they, too, will have justice. They will experience what real justice can be. Jesus knew this when he spoke those words. He saw the injustice that was about him in the part of the world in which he lived, and he knew where strict justice was eventually to be found—in the spirit world.

But he also knew that mercy does not come from God but from man to fellow man. It is the theologians who have built up this singular conception of the Father. It is they who have transmogrified the Great Father into a stern and awful judge.

Depart from me, ye cursed, into everlasting fire, which was prepared for the devil and all his angels. Here in the gospel we are supposed to have the very words with which God will condemn the transgressor. In the spirit world, it fills us with unspeakable horror to contemplate upon the enormity of any person authoritatively teaching others that the Father of us all could utter words of such fearful condemnation. And these words are put into the mouth of Jesus, although it must be conceded that, at long last, honest doubts are creeping into the minds of churchmen on earth that so much that Jesus is reputed to have said was, in good truth, never spoken by him at all.

Assuredly this evil sentence upon the transgressor must be placed first upon the list of utterances that were never made by Jesus. Indeed, he could not have given voice to such downright, unblushing falsehood. For there is not one atom of truth in it. Nor is there any truth whatever in any statement appearing in the New Testament wherein it is specifically asserted that man shall be condemned for all eternity, no matter how great may be the enormity of his 'sins'.

There is no awful Judgement Day, whether it be alleged to take place immediately upon man's passing into the spirit world or at some later and unspecified time. I have said this to you before. At the risk of being tiresome, I cannot refrain from repeating it.

The dread of Judgement Day—or of being summoned before the High Court of Heaven to be judged and sentenced—either or both of these outrageous beliefs have cast a blight upon the whole earth world for hundreds of earthly years. It has filled many, many estimable souls with the uttermost despondency. Many others with sensitive minds have passed their earthly lives in a state of spiritual terror because of that dread day that is supposed to await them at the close of their earthly lives.

It is part of my work in the spirit world to be at hand when people are making their entrance into these lands as residents, so that I speak from first-hand experience when I tell you of the abject terror that consumes so many poor souls when their moment of transition has come. Instead of the winter of their earthly lives passing gently into the glorious fresh, fragrant spring of their new life in these lands, they arrive here with that terror full upon them. Such beliefs are relics of pure paganism, but this wicked fiction has been kept up and disseminated by the Churches of earth as a measure of inspiring fear into the hearts of their 'faithful'. As a former priest of the Church, I regret, deeply and earnestly, that I ever gave tongue to such misguided teaching. And there are hosts of others like me.

Man has been branded by the theologians as something so evil; so much accent has been laid upon '*sinful*' man, and the Father of the universe is alleged to be so stern and awful (always the Great Dread Judge), that there is little wonder that man upon the earth-plane turns with some hope, forlorn though it may be, to the mercy that might be given to him.

The most that the average man can do upon earth is to hope for the best, to hope that perhaps things may not be so terrible for him in the afterlife as he has been led to believe. He has no certainty of it, and the Church would say that he has no right to assume anything, but he can sometimes think quietly. And out of those quiet thoughts he may derive some measure of spiritual insight; he may receive a little inspiration from some unseen friend of the spirit world—and leave the theologians and official spiritual teachers to their incomprehensible creeds and dogmas and their spiritual presumption. For no one is more presumptuous than the theologian, who, knowing little or nothing of the truth of spiritual matters, professes to know a great deal.

Fear is the strongest weapon, the deadliest weapon, in the theological armoury. For hundreds of years Orthodoxy has wielded this weapon to inspire fear in the hearts of Mankind—by the supposed dire penalties which it will be their misfortune to suffer when they pass to the 'next world' if they should have misbehaved themselves on earth. The worst sentence of all is to be condemned to hell for all eternity where the 'sinner' will remain forever in strange fires that burn but never consume.

But let it not be assumed that there is not a day of reckoning for all mankind. Most assuredly there is. And that moment first presents itself immediately we have cast off the physical body in 'death'. Thence forward. Every day—to use earthly terms—every moment of the day, becomes our time of reckoning. We judge ourselves as we go along in life in the spirit world. We do not hold a formal court of inquiry into our actions as we proceed in our life, but the inevitable law of cause and effect, being ever operative, provides us with the very essence of progression. We ourselves provide the cause; we thus set the law in motion. And the law produces the effect. That is how we progress in the spirit world. There is none to judge us but ourselves, and we can be stern and unrelenting to ourselves!

I want to make myself perfectly clear when I say that man judges himself. I am not speaking figuratively, neither am I suggesting that as each soul arrives in the spirit world it becomes so enlightened that it immediately perceives with full comprehension all the errors of its life. If that were so it would not be long before the dark realms and the grey lands were soon emptied of their inhabitants. I mean simply this: the law of cause and effect is in continual, perpetual operation upon every person who is born upon earth from the moment of his drawing breath upon that plane of existence, right through his earthly life, and so it continues after he has passed here into the spirit world. The operation of that law is, in its effect, precisely the same as though a complete process of adjudication were set in motion under the presidency of some individual. That is exactly what *has* happened, the individual who is presiding being ourselves.

Let us consider a simple analogy. If we should choose voluntarily to plunge our hand into the blaze of a red-hot fire, we should suffer the most excruciating agony from our burnt fingers. Could we blame a single soul for our most foolhardy action? Most certainly not, for what we did, we did of our own free will. We were fully aware that it was a mad act to commit, but we persisted none the less. Could we blame the fire for burning us? Again, most certainly not for it is the nature of fire to burn, and it is simply the operation of cause and effect.

My analogy is but an elementary one, but it has its direct application, because a misspent life, a life lived upon earth in a series of transgressions, will have the same effect upon us—an effect which will be fully revealed when we arrive in the spirit world—as though we had thrust our hand into the flames of the fire. We see what we have done; we see the result of what we have done.

We see where the blame rests; we see just what we have done for ourselves. We perceive unerringly that it is our own fault, the fault of no one else, and therefore we can blame no one else. What we did, we did deliberately and of our own free will. Our motive was bad, or, alternatively, our motive was not good. Applying this rule to our earthly lives, for it is with our earthly lives I am treating at the moment, you will observe just where God enters into our true spiritual appraisement. *He enters nowhere.* He is not judging us; He will not judge us, either at the moment of our transition or at some unknown later date. There is, in fact, no need for Him—or for anyone else—to do the judging. We shall be compelled to do it most efficiently ourselves.

To return to my analogy. We have but to gaze upon our burnt hand for the whole story to reveal itself to our minds with full truth. Others, too, can see the dreadful burns, but they need not know how they were brought about. We are under no obligation to tell them, but there will come a time when we shall be glad to unburden our troubled minds of its load of misery and sadness.

Lest some of my good friends upon earth should take me too literally, or mistakenly to misapply my little analogy, let me hasten to assure them that there are no flames here in the spirit world. Those dreadful flames of hell do not have any place in the economics of the spirit world!

I am speaking to you at some length upon this particular subject of Judgement and Judgement Day because I have in mind my own earthly experiences, from which I know, as do you, the universal extent of the belief and the fear which it inspires. I want to remove that fear if possible, and in doing so to bring some brightness and gladness into the lives and thoughts of my good friends upon earth. But most of all, it is my greatest wish that my friends should have a better and deeper understanding of the Great Father of the universe since it is He whom the orthodox religions of the earth traduce so abominably and outrageously in their transforming Him into a grim and horrifying Judge, from whom our principal hope is mercy.

From our discussion of justice and mercy, one or two subsidiary questions may come into your mind, which it is opportune to answer now. For instance, you might ask: how does justice actually operate in the spirit world? Justice, as we know it on earth, must be dispensed by someone or other. It cannot come about of itself if we are considering some particular cause.

Now that, my good friend, is a difficult question to answer unless one should be a spiritual expert or technician. Suppose I were to ask you how did the fire burn that hand? Of what is the flame composed and how does it burn? There I think we should find ourselves both in the same relative position. We can most of us say what happens in particular cases, and we can be very familiar with certain effects, but we are not all conversant with the actual forces that are set in motion, nor how they operate. We can, however, throw a little light upon this matter.

Justice, as we are now considering it, is a very comprehensive term. In the spirit world it means that not only shall the transgressor receive his just merits, it means also that all who have suffered during their earthly lives, whether from the evil deeds of others or from stress of adverse circumstances, or from illness and defects of the physical body, all such people shall be accorded a full measure of compensation through the natural means which are abundant and lavish in spirit lands. Justice, you will see, will be given to those who have suffered through the fault of no one.

A long chain of circumstances and events might have led to the eventual afflictions of one individual, but justice will be done to that person freely and fully. Perhaps you already have knowledge of some of the manifold delights which are to be found in these realms of light, and the supreme joy which they bring to all of us here, and will bring to the thousands who in future time are bound for these realms. Therein lies their compensation for everything which they might have endured, and I have yet to find anyone who is not in whole-hearted agreement with me that the happiness that is to be derived here far outweighs any and every unhappiness that was ours during our earthly lives. The incarnate need have no fear upon that score. Compensation is lavishly bestowed. But there is also the justice that comes to the evil-doer.

The acts and thoughts of our earthly lives are registered within us, and thus our life's history is indelibly recorded within our never-failing memories. In order to understand this you must first of all know one simple fact of spiritual knowledge. It is this: spirituality means light; the absence of spirituality means darkness. I am not speaking figuratively, but literally. The light is *real* light, just as you have on earth in the noonday of summer, and is not some 'spiritual experience'. The darkness is Stygian, the complete absence of light, and it can be blacker even than the darkness of the darkest midnight of a bleak and bitter winter on earth, or of some deep tenebrous dungeon below the ground.

The individuals who live in these two contrasting states of light and darkness exactly match their surroundings of brightness and gloom in their own persons. Their bodies and their very raiment will correspond minutely with their habitation. In the bright realms, wherein it is my happy fortune to live, our clothing and our physical frames are as full of light as are our surroundings. The same state of things exists in the greater and more exalted realms above us to a degree that is indescribable in ordinary earthly terms. In addition, the very countenances of the elevated beings who inhabit those realms have taken upon their lineaments the high spirituality of their realms.

In the dark realms, the reverse takes place. The denizens are hideous in form and feature, distorted sometimes out of all resemblance to their once human appearance. Indeed, when they were upon earth they may have been elegant in form and handsome in feature, but are now reduced to their true status. Their attire may be filthy rags, a mere mockery of clothing. They may present such a revolting spectacle that one would naturally recoil from contact with them. The base deeds of their lives have reacted upon them, both in body and mind. They possess no perceptible glimmer of *light* themselves, and their habitation is similarly devoid of light. You will see my meaning when I repeat that spirituality means light, the absence of spirituality means darkness.

You will also observe the monumental stupidity of Orthodoxy when, in its blindness, it pontifically pronounces that when we of the spirit world return to earth to speak with our friends there, we are nothing but *devils of hell masquerading as angels of light!* There is no such masquerading here, I do assure you, my good friend.

Nowhere in the spirit world is it possible for any person, of whatever description, to assume one scintilla of light which is not completely and absolutely his own. No person can endow another with light, temporarily or permanently. The light which emanates from us is the result of the working of the law of cause and effect—which is justice.

Another question which may come to your mind is this: how does each person go, automatically, as it seems, to the exact place he has earned for himself? Who decides the matter?

To answer the last question first: no one decides the matter for any person; the person decides it for himself. He goes automatically to his right abode because that is the abode for which he is exactly fitted. He is attuned to that abode in a manner which I will explain to you. For the same reason, there is no fear of an individual over-stepping or escaping from the dark realms if so be it he has condemned himself to those regions. The reason is this: the kind of life which every soul leads upon earth reacts directly upon his spiritual counterpart; in other words, a person's spirit body will possess just that degree of light which is resultant from his life on earth.

If his life has been bad in every sense, then his spirit body will possess little or no light. The sphere to which he goes in the spirit world will possess exactly the same degree of light as the spirit body itself, no more, no less. The two coincide perfectly; they are attuned.

We might draw a simple analogy from the oceans of the earth world. The sea, as you must know, is comprised of water of various densities in which myriads of creatures are living, segregated according to the different densities. They are fitted for the particular pressure of water by their physical construction. If, broadly speaking, creatures occupying water of one density attempted to enter that of another density, they would bring destruction upon themselves if they penetrated far enough. They would be forewarned of any encroachment or deviation from their rightful sphere by acute discomfort or suffering.

The barriers between these different densities are invisible, but they are there none the less. Now if we leave the ocean and come to dry land. we find that human beings will suffer acute distress and might even terminate their earthly life abruptly if they penetrate into regions of atmospheric pressure to which they are not accustomed, or for which they are unprovided with special apparatus with which to counterbalance such unaccustomed atmospheric density.

Perhaps you would find great difficulty in breathing when upon the heights of a lofty mountain. When venturing into high altitudes in the air, you must be fully protected or your earthly life will quickly terminate. Again, the barriers are invisible, but none the less real. So it is in the spirit world. In the dark regions of the spirit world the Density—if so we might call it—is enormous as you would compute such things. Inhabitants of higher realms can enter them only when suitably protected by the necessary spiritual 'apparatus'. I use the term 'apparatus' in a figurative sense only. We do not actually wear any special clothing or other impedimenta for the purpose. The particular protection that is needed is afforded through our mental abilities. We must all learn how to perform this mental process before we venture into the dark realms, and even then an experienced cicerone is indispensable.

When we are invited to pay a visit to realms higher than that which we normally inhabit, some dweller in the higher realm will always be present to equip us for the journey. That is a process which we cannot undertake to do for ourselves since it needs extra force which we do not ourselves possess.

When we walk across our own particular realm we shall eventually come to a spot or locality where we shall feel that we are not as comfortable as we were. We shall see and feel the light becoming stronger, and we shall be unable to withstand it. That is one of the invisible barriers of the realm. (Increased intensity of light may not, *per se*, constitute a barrier). That is where the relative density is beginning to change.

So it is throughout the whole vast dominion of the spirit world. We shall each dwell in that region where we feel most comfortable. Even in the dark realms that rule applies, although it may sound strange to your earthly ears to speak of comfort in those revolting regions. But whatever distress comes to a soul in darkness, it is not so much from the realm in which he lives as from the mental state into which he is plunged. The realm itself does not inflict tortures upon him. His fellow beings alone do that. He is not inevitably condemned to live there; his own spiritual state will keep him there until such time as he feels the urge to progress.

Thus, you will plainly see that justice in the spirit world is the operation of the law of cause and effect, and that it requires no administrator but ourselves alone. We have inflicted upon ourselves the condition in which we find ourselves. To whom can we cry for mercy? The forgiveness which we may receive from another will carry us no further on the way. We pay the price to the uttermost farthing. Our wounds are self-inflicted; we can blame none but ourselves. The Father of Heaven has not judged us; He has not condemned us; we have not offended Him; He has nothing to forgive us. We have broken spiritual laws, that, and that only. Why should we beg for mercy? What right have we to beg for mercy? We knew that fire scorches and burns—to return to our old analogy—yet we deliberately plunged our hands into the flames.

Blessed are the merciful *on earth*. Blessed are they that seek justice for they shall have their fill *in the spirit world*.

Prayer

I have constantly emphasised, I hope not to the point of being tedious, that in the spirit world we do not live in a perpetual state of spiritual ecstasy nor are we existing in an atmosphere of perfervid religious emotion with life one never-ending cycle of 'prayer and praise' and singing of 'psalms, and hymns, and spiritual canticles' offered up in unceasing flow to the 'great throne'.

We are not what the earth-plane would call religious minded for the *very* simple reason that we have no religion as it is known—but scarcely understood—in the earth world.

I have been keenly sensitive of the urgent need to stress these points because they affect the whole outlook of so many people of the earth world in their regard of the spirit world.

Orthodox religion is to blame for this misconception because orthodox religion, in its diversified doctrinal claims and dogmatic asseverations, has assumed to itself so many exclusive rights over the spirit world. It has taken charge of the soul whilst it is on earth, and it has endeavoured to show mankind how to live its earthly life—while often showing a poor example in its own behaviour. It has made many monstrous claims in respect of its knowledge and power, both of which virtually amount to nothing, and by pure theological speculation based upon New Testament 'interpretation', together with the faulty opinions of early churchmen, it professes to forecast the almost exact spiritual condition of a soul after it has passed into the spirit world. A clear case of the blind leading the blind.

The orthodox church has tried to make the spirit world into a 'religious' place or state, the religious element being principally Christian, if not wholly so. Many people earnestly believe that the non-Christian will *become* Christian when he leaves the earth-plane for the spirit world so that in the end the spirit world will be one vast assembly of undisputed and irreproachable Christians! Some necessary adjustment would have to be made, of course, to bring into harmony all the various and antagonistic creeds, but that, no doubt, will be easily accomplished by the providential organisation of the greater world of the spirit. The most dogmatic of earthly religions sees the spirit world only in terms of its own dogmatism, and all must, therefore, yield to the truths of which it believes itself to be the sole depository on earth.

This strange conception of the spirit world as being one enormous temple of prayer, as it were, where the inmates of 'heaven' dwell in a state of holiness and piety, is a conception that is as far removed from the truth as the light of day is from the darkness of night, as I have tried to show you. The imagination recoils from contemplating such a state of existence for all eternity.

No mind could possibly survive the ordeal of an eternity of prayer alone, even with the monotony relieved in some measure by the singing of hymns and spiritual songs.

By prayer, of course, I mean that type of prayer in use in the churches on the earth-plane and that are to be found in the ordinary printed prayer books. Prayer, like so much else that concerns man's spiritual welfare, has been moulded and modelled by unimaginative minds of the earth-plane upon an entirely preposterous conception of the Father of the universe.

Never was this grotesque conception more clearly exemplified than in the volumes of prayers that have been composed for the members of all earthly religions. As we see it in the spirit world, the *motif* of most of the prayers in such books is pure paganism. The fulsome adulation with which the Father of the universe is addressed, the extreme degree of self-abasement that is expressed by the one who is praying, are begotten of a nervous fear and dread of the 'unknown hereafter'. High-sounding words, long grandiloquent phrases, and the recital of a wide variety of abstruse doctrinal beliefs, are put into the mouths of folk in prayer who have no notion of what they are saying, and which, in any case, have little application to their simple lives.

Many earth people have been tortured by such prayers for generations because the very substance of these prayers has created fear in their minds. A sensitive mind will inwardly become haunted by his own seeming unworthiness—as detailed and emphasised by the prayer-books—ever to come within a thousand thousand miles of 'heaven'.

He is constantly being forced to say, if he uses a prayerbook, that he is the most miserable of sinners. A sensitive soul will believe such a description of himself. A person of another type of mind will not believe one word of it, but will repeat the statement just the same. In the first case, it will have the worst possible effect upon the mind; in the second case it is senseless, where it is not sheer hypocrisy.

In the spirit world we are in a position to see the value, the efficacy, of certain set forms of prayer whether they be the private devotions of ordinary individuals or the prayers that are incorporated in church services.

Let me say at once that prayer-books used as a vehicle of private devotions are as a rule of no value whatever. In too numerous instances the prayers are based upon beliefs which have no foundation in the truth. There has always seemed to be a fixed idea in the minds of those who compose the prayers that a constant recital of what are fondly believed to be the singular attributes of the Father of Heaven is to Him the most acceptable form of prayer. Most prayers open with such adulation and close with an utterly meaningless statement of some doctrinal belief.

Basically, prayer is a concentration of thought directed to the Father of the universe. We will leave for the moment the particular intention of prayer in any specific case, and we will discuss prayer in general.

In the spirit world, thought has a tangible effect. It is visible to us where it is invisible to you. You can never see the immediate effect of your thoughts. Here in the spirit world, we always do. Although we can speak to one another through the medium of sound just in the same way as do you upon the earth-plane, our best-liked and generally adopted method of personal communication is by the thought process.

One of my earliest experiences in company with my friends, Edwin and Ruth (the former of whom met me upon my transition), was when Edwin spoke to Ruth and me from some distance away. Hitherto we had used our earthly method of speech. But now a light flashed before us, and we heard the sound of Edwin's voice speaking clearly to us. His thought had travelled to us instantaneously, and we fully understood it, just as you understand each other's voices upon the earth-plane.

Edwin's thoughts had passed to us unfailingly and unerringly, and so we had received them. Now this function of thought transference is not confined exclusively to inhabitants of the spirit world nor are we the only people who are able to practise it. Every human being can do so. It is possible—and perfectly natural—for people still living in the earth world to direct their thoughts to some friend in the spirit world, and they are always doing so. If those thoughts are directed with the full intention that they should be received by the person concerned, then received they will be, beyond any doubt whatever.

In the reverse direction, we can send our thoughts to you. They will be bound to reach you, but unless you are sufficiently sensitive psychically you will not be aware of receiving them, or on receiving them, you will not be aware whence they have come. Many people will just consider that some relevant or irrelevant thought has 'come into their head'.

In the spirit world, thought is not necessarily seen, as it were, in transit. If that were so the whole of the spirit realms would be criss-crossed with a maze of coloured shafts of light of varying degrees of intensity and colour.

While such an effect might be curious, and, indeed, pretty to look upon at first sight, after a time it would become too distracting and confusing to the mind. Thought, therefore, is mostly invisible in transit.

But the *results* of certain concentrations of thought can be felt by us all here in a collective sense. During times of festivity on the earth-plane, such, for example, as at Christmas-tide, when in normal times the earth world breaths forth the greatest measure of goodwill, and when many folks' minds turn towards their friends in the spirit lands, during such festive periods we are keenly aware of a great ascension of kindly thoughts. Such thoughts spread themselves over these realms like a great mantle of affection and joyousness.

That is the result of combined efforts of thought. Now prayer operates in precisely the same way as the two forms of concentrated thought which I have just outlined to you—personal thoughts directed to a friend and general thoughts sent out into the spirit world to a number of friends upon some special occasion.

In these two instances we have the exact parallel of private prayer and public prayer or 'worship'. And they are both dependent upon one and the same indispensable condition. The thoughts, whether private or collective, *must,* without failure, be positively directed to the person or persons for whom they are intended. If we do not receive your thoughts it is because you have not directed them with firm and precise intention.

We, as the percipients, are blameless in the matter. We might receive but half of your thought, the remainder having no motive power behind it because the mind has wandered along other paths, and thus the full thought has failed to reach us. Those of us who are in active communion with our friends upon the earth-plane enjoy many a good laugh when some friend starts to speak to us clearly and coherently, only for the thought to become weaker and weaker, finally to ramble off into silence. If you could see this happening, I know you would laugh too!

However, in passing, let me say that we can often guess the remainder by filling in the omissions for ourselves. Or perhaps we might send back an answering thought for you to 'clear the line' to allow your thoughts an unobstructed path.

Such distractions are perfectly common—and perfectly natural—in the earth world, but they can be obviated in a very simple manner, and that is by retreating from them; by retiring to some place where you will be untroubled by them, where you can forget yourselves and your surroundings in some measure, and so leave your minds free to perform their office of thought concentration and direction. You should, also, assume as easy and comfortable a posture as possible for the physical body since any physical discomfort is as disturbing as any other distraction. It is true you can direct your thoughts to us while you are out of doors upon the road, but we frown upon such times and places, and discourage them because of the dangers which are daily to be encountered upon the public highways of the earth.

Your thoughts, then, can be directed to us at any moment and from any place where you should happen to be situated. In circumstances of distress, trouble, or perplexity, place and conditions have no inhibiting influence because the stimulus to the mind occasioned by distress will provide sufficient directive force to the thought. But for all normal purposes where you wish to send your thought to us here, quiet and repose are the surest means of success.

The repose should be both of the physical body itself and of the mind. Acquire the first and it will be easier to acquire the second. Remember this, and remember also that the essence of successful thought transmission is to keep always in mind the person who is being addressed, and you will understand how it is that we in the spirit world have such a poor opinion of much that goes on in the churches of the earth-plane under the designation of prayer.

My friends and I have made special journeys to the earth world to observe the effect, under varying conditions, of different services taking place in the churches. We have been enabled to see exactly what each individual—including the officiating minister—has put forth as an effort of prayer. In the great majority of cases, the results, alas, have been negligible.

On so many occasions the thoughts of the congregation were obviously wandering far from the purpose for which the people were assembled. The minister was performing his share of the service in a purely mechanical fashion, begotten of long practice and complete familiarity. He was thus able to conduct his part of the service without in the least having to think about what he was saying. He read from his service books the words that were printed there, and he earned out certain actions that were required by the ritual or order of the service.

Seldom could we perceive any spiritual thoughts being emitted by the minister such as we should have done. We ought to have observed a flash of light as his thoughts left him to ascend to Him to Whom they were directed. But most of all, we should have seen the downpouring of celestial rays that would have indicated beyond all doubt that the prayers had been properly directed, had been received, and that they were being accorded their full acknowledgment. Had the thoughts of the whole congregation, there assembled, been adequately concentrated and emitted, the whole building would have become bathed in the most thrilling galaxy of celestial colours and blends of colours.

Supposing the fervour of the congregation to have gradually increased—though this is hardly to be expected in most earthly churches—we should have beheld an immense thought-form of the most beautiful shape and colour to have enveloped the entire church, to soar up and up into the highest empyrean, a magnificent manifestation of the power of spiritual thought directed to the Great Source of all. But no; we saw none of these things. What we did see was a feeble flicker of light as someone tried to marshal his thoughts, a flicker that quickly died down and disappeared, leaving the surroundings in the same state of spiritual gloom as they were before.

And the cause? There are several. Chief among them is the very form of the services themselves. Long, inappropriate recitations from dull and dreary psalms have no spiritual value whatever. The oral recounting of incidents and acts that took place some two thousand years ago are of no help spiritually. But the recital of prayers so familiar that they can be said without any effort of will at all, leaving the mind free to think of what it likes—and that anything but the object in hand; the recital of prayers, the contents of which have little or no interest for, nor application to, the one who is praying; the repetition of incomprehensible creeds, and the droning of versicles and responses by people who are heedless of what they are saying—just ponder these matters.

Then consider the cringing attitude of mind that is instilled into the churchgoer when he is told that at best he is a 'miserable sinner'; and consider, too, the general air of appeasement to a wrathful God who, supposedly, will bring down condign punishment upon humanity if it misbehaves itself, together with the abject self-abasement that this same strange God demands as His strict right—just contemplate all this, and then ask yourself, my dear friend: is it to be wondered at that those few churches we visited were just places of grey gloom, whence few prayers, real prayers, ever ascended to the high realms of heaven?

What of our personal devotions, you will say, the prayers that we say at home in the privacy of our room? If the formulae of the prayer-books can be discarded, then real prayers will have some chance of being said, to the everlasting benefit of the person who says them. But they must be real sensible efforts of thought.

First of all, let us forget altogether the stereotyped form of prayer that is familiar to most people, some characteristics of which I have just given you. Let us start afresh, as it were, as though we were approaching the matter for the first time, and so with our minds perfectly free from any conventional notions.

Prayer is a grand, sturdy, virile thing, not a cringing, crawling, sanctimonious affair. In our prayers we have something to say. Let us say it in a wholesome, forthright fashion. Let us, of course, show our respect by the courteous way in which we frame our thoughts. We need not use long, ponderous phrases, nor need we use an extreme preciosity in choosing our words. We need not, if we wish, employ the rather picturesque, though archaic mode of address in our use of 'Thou' and 'Thee'. It is not in the least necessary, and its absence in no way connotes a want of respect and reverence.

Your prayers should be the clothing of your thoughts in words, since it is natural for you on the earth-plane to transform your thoughts mentally into words. The shortest prayer, consisting of only a few words sincerely intended, with the thought fully concentrated and powerfully directed, is far, far better than the grandest, most rhetorical prayer that was ever uttered, if the latter should be merely so many words with scarcely any meaning, without intention, and with no directive force behind it.

Such a 'prayer', in fact, is simply a waste of time. Some of the finest prayers are also the simplest and the shortest. There are not many people upon the earth-plane who are able to sustain a prolonged effort of thought directed in prayer. Whatever happens, their minds are bound to wander, sooner or later, and the prayer at once becomes non-existent. With the motive power withdrawn it will never reach its high destination, nor, indeed, any destination at all!

The most efficacious prayer is that from which is eliminated any fulsome flattering recital of the Great Father's attributes. It is a pure survival of paganism and superstition, and it is utterly worthless. It reeks of sycophancy. It suggests that we must first flatter the Father of the universe as a form of approach before we make Him a request and judging by the usual lengthy preamble in this fashion that forms the opening to so many of the earth world's formal prayers, the greater the flattery, the greater are the chances of having the prayer answered!

So many earth people cease to be themselves truly, when they essay to pray. They seem to think that a prayerbook is essential, because, presumably in the eyes of the compilers of prayer-books, they are completely incapable of expressing themselves upon any subject whatever. They believe that an earnest request for help and guidance must be worded in great lengthy periods more formal and grandiose and ponderous than the most involved state document of ancient days! In short, your prayers should be just as homely, simple, and informal in their construction as your conversation among your friends, sincere and heartfelt, and shorn of affectations which are not natural to you. And I would add, let them be brief!

You are much more likely to be successful with brevity. Of course, you will appreciate that we are not here considering such circumstances as of your being in dire trouble where the only relief and hope in your mind resides in a protracted outpouring of your troubles to the Great Father. In such cases the circumstances are altogether different.

In successful prayer, whether it is said by you upon the earth-plane, or by us here in the spirit world, the result, is a perfect linking up with the Father of the universe and ourselves. The response will be the same whether we be in church or out of it. But prayer has a much larger field than is contained within the boundaries with which the people of the earth-plane usually circumscribe it.

Prayer in its wider sense can spring from our mind spontaneously, aroused from the conditions or circumstances of the moment. The glories of the universe are ever about us here in the spirit world. I have told you of some of them. The joy, for example, that the beholding of beautiful flowers will bring to us becomes in our minds a *Te Deum* of thanksgiving which we send to the Creator of all such delights.

We do not give such thoughts any formal shape: we do not express ourselves in so many thought-words. But we do know we are for ever grateful for what is giving us this great joy and that is prayer also. You can readily imagine how these realms are rendered still more beautiful by the downpouring of light that everlastingly descends upon us in response to our thoughts of happiness and gratefulness.

We need no elaborate ritual or ceremonial to convey our gratitude to the Father of the universe for the bounties He so richly showers down upon us. We do not find ourselves tongue-tied and obliged to have recourse to the printed words of prayer-books. We do not need to assume that most inhibiting of all postures—kneeling—when we wish to send our thoughts aloft.

We just transmit our thoughts of the moment, wherever we are and whatever we may be doing. Our enjoyment of the vast beauties of these realms, and the happiness which every single tiny element brings to us, are themselves a prayer to Him who gives them to us. In whatsoever we rejoice, according to our particular tastes and predilections, that rejoicing is an unspoken prayer, but a real prayer, none the less.

The state of happiness in which we in these realms are living is ever continuous. It never loses its savour by its constant presence. Our happiness never becomes stale, if I may so express it. It is an emotion of which we are for ever aware, and the very consciousness of our happiness is transformed into an unexpressed prayer. Though unexpressed in so many words, it is powerful, and the great Giver of these delights receives and responds to our unspoken prayer.

By an outrageous perversion of the truth, the earthly Church teaches that God *demands as His right* that all good people shall worship Him, and praise Him, and thank Him for what He has done for them. Were such a shocking fiction even remotely true, how many people of the earth could possibly do any of these things when the picture of the Father of Heaven as painted for you by the Church is such a gross travesty? The Father of Heaven *demands* nothing of His children, whether they be of the earth world or of the spirit world. He does not demand 'worship', or praise, or thanks. *He does not even ask for them.*

The beauties of these realms of the spirit world are living things. They respond to our love of them and thereby they become still more beautiful. But the power behind all this beauty comes from One Being only, and we are ever conscious of it. Being thus conscious of it, our feelings of gratitude are always with us. These feelings of gratitude are translated into thoughts of thanksgiving, and in our minds we glorify the Giver, freely, without being told that we *must* do so.

We magnify the Name of the Giver freely, without being told that He will be wrathful if we do not observe what He demands of us. The 'worship' that we give Him is the 'worship' of true affection, and not the bowing down to an Unknown God, whom the earth world is taught *to* fear, and Who demands 'worship' from His children as His right.

Had the earth world not lived in spiritual blindness for so many hundreds of years, the inhabitants of it would by now know something of the rudiments of praying. They would know how to go about it without choking it with false doctrines, with sickly religious sentiment, with sanctimoniousness. They would know that true prayer is not a matter of a clergyman intoning in a pleasant voice, nor the gabbling of long extracts from the ancient writers.

Knowing the proper method of saying prayers, the whole earth world would have benefited. The fact that prayer is regarded by so many earth people as a pious practice for those inclined towards 'religion' has been brought about by the parody under which so much passes for real prayer. Prayer can be—and is—separated entirely from anything even remotely approaching organised religion. That is how we use prayer in the spirit world. The earth world could do precisely the same if it chose to do so.

The Lord's Prayer

A moment ago I referred to prayers which are so familiar that they can be recited from memory and without any effort of will, leaving the mind to think of whatever it likes. Of all such prayers, I am inclined to believe that the Lord's Prayer is the most often said under such conditions.

It has long been claimed that it is one of the most perfect of prayers, not only because it was given by Jesus himself, but because so much is contained within the compass of so few words. But whatever force the prayer might have is completely nullified by its customary thoughtless recital.

There would seem to have become attached to the Lord's Prayer, in the minds of thousands of people, some sort of talismanic power. It usually has a place in most of the organised recitals of prayers, seemingly by virtue of some prescriptive right, as though the efficacy of any church service or private devotions would be greatly impaired if it were omitted.

Now the very fact of its being so well known on earth that it can be recited by heart is also the measure—or at least one measure—of its *inefficacy,* for reasons that we have seen, namely, the lack of mental concentration upon what is being said. That is fatal to any and every prayer from the most sublime invocation to the most simple. The mind *must* be focused upon what is being said; the person who prays *must know and understand* exactly what he is saying, so that both knowing and understanding he can give sufficient directive force to his words and thoughts.

It is really astonishing, as we see things from the spirit world, how many people fondly imagine that the bare repetition of words such as are contained, for instance, in the Lord's Prayer, is alone necessary to achieve its purpose. It is such folk who believe that this particular prayer (and others of a similar order) carries with it some magic power of its own. They may think that because it is extracted from the Scriptures, it will have some added property that no prayer composed by an ordinary person can possibly have. So it is that this prayer has been elevated to the front rank of all set invocations.

Let us, then, view the Lord's Prayer from the standpoint of the spirit world.

Firstly, I would say that in so far as my experience of these realms is concerned, it is a prayer that we never employ. The principal reason for this is that the sentiment contained within it does not apply to us here. Another reason is that we *seldom or never* make use of prescribed or stereotype prayers.

Before we proceed further, I must make it clear that whoever composed this prayer, Jesus, with his great spiritual knowledge, was not the author of it.

Jesus is presumed to have suggested to his hearer that they should pray 'after this manner', not necessarily using the words he gave, but after the fashion which he then proceeded to exemplify.

The first feature we notice is brevity. The next is that the opening of the prayer is devoid of extravagant, excessive, and perforce, insincere adulation of the Father of Heaven, addressed specifically to Himself. I have already spoken of this to you, and here in this prayer we have an ideal opening.

Can it seriously be thought and believed that God

would actually take pleasure in listening to the recitation of a long catalogue of His supposed superlative qualities?

I say *supposed* qualities because so much is attributed to the Great Father that has its origin in a total misconception of Him. The adjectival preambles of most of the earth world's prayers are but a survival of paganism, when people worshipped gods of varying descriptions and of uncertain temper.

The 'faithful' of those remote days attributed most things to their deities; personal and national misfortunes, storms and other meteorological disturbances of whatever nature, all were ascribed to the wrath of the gods. It became vitally necessary, therefore, to address their deities in terms which they considered would please them most, thus throwing them into a good humour and placating them generally.

They were under the delusion that what a god likes to hear most is a recital of his own sterling qualities. Once a pleasant relationship were thus established, the real object of the prayer could be proceeded with. This relic of paganism is still resident in the minds of a great host of folk upon earth, and never more so than among Orthodoxy and its exponents. The composers of prayers have followed this tradition.

The Lord's Prayer, then, commences with the brief *hallowed be Thy name*. Even this is not essential. It could easily be omitted from any prayer without impairing the value of it whatever.

Thy kingdom come is a phrase that means nothing in the minds of most people. They say it because it is included in the prayer, and therefore its value is upon the same level as so much else which is nothing more than mere theology. Churchmen teach that these words are the expression of hope that all men will come to know God, and that God's spiritual kingdom may be spread throughout the world. The very vagueness of the whole 'interpretation' is revealed in its terms.

Theologians will contend that the universality of God's kingdom can only come about through the spreading of the Christian religion. The latter then becomes the standard of spiritual knowledge and spiritual teaching by which the whole earth shall be governed, and the religious and secular affairs of its people conducted. The life that follows after 'death' will be a Christian life, to be lived in all the perfection of true religious thought and knowledge as gained through the Christian religion.

Doubts are, of course, entertained concerning the fate of the 'heathen', the 'unbaptised', and, without doubt, those who practise communication with the spirit world. These latter folk are oftimes regarded as beyond all hope! How are ecclesiastics to know—unless they have taken the trouble to ascertain—that the spirit world is not an exclusively Christian world; that its inhabitants are here in these and other realms regardless of whether they were Christians or not; that the fact of their being Christian or not is a matter that is never inquired into, never heeded even; that whether they were Christians, or not, makes not the slightest difference to their spiritual status and the welcome they receive here in these realms, not the least difference to their spiritual prospects or means of attaining spiritual evolution and progression?

How are people, especially the orthodox teachers of the earth world, to know if they never trouble to find out that the spirit world contains in these realms of light, as well as in higher and lower states, individuals who, collectively, held every shade of non-Christian thought when they were incarnate? To pray, then, that the Christian religion may be spread throughout the whole face of the earth is not necessarily a good thing because orthodox Christianity embodies within it so much that is absolutely false. It will bolster up and support systems of living that are unquestionably wrong as we see things in these realms.

The historical record of organised Christianity is not a good one. The list of people who have had their earthly lives violently terminated in the name of Christianity is a horrible one. There is scarcely a religious denomination upon earth that does not claim its role of 'martyrs for the faith', whose transitions were encompassed by opposing sects. The 'kingdom of God' does not include religious teaching accompanied by force; it does not include religious persecution; it does not countenance the use of the word *heretic:* it does not, in fact, include much of what is in the minds of ecclesiastics when they hope for the coming of this kingdom.

It is even believed by doctors of the Church that the kingdom of God, when fully established, will witness the complete overthrow of Satan, and sin will thus be banished from the earth. Such beliefs as these are childishly crude. I freely confess that once I believed these things myself when I was incarnate, and taught them. But those days are passed, and I am now a happy resident of the spirit world where we can see the precise value of so much that we embraced as religious beliefs before we came to dwell in these lands. 'Very well, then,' I hear it objected, 'Tell us precisely what is the kingdom of God.'

Now you are asking me to explain something that has been invented by the earth world. It is rather you who should explain to *me* just what is meant by it. Beyond what I have given you as to its interpretation by churchmen, there is nothing that can be added that is of any consequence in further exposition. Later on I will suggest something to you that will, perhaps, throw a little light upon the joint relationship of our two worlds, yours and mine, and which might, if you wish so to regard it, be considered as giving some substance to the words *Thy kingdom come.*

Thy will be done. In this brief phrase is bound up the very essence of the whole prayer because it is taught and believed upon earth that one's prayers are answered or remain unanswered according to God's will. Indeed, the will of God is brought forward upon every occasion when some religious 'mystery' presents itself. A prayer is not answered, therefore it is because God's will ordains that it should not be answered. We are not worthy that it should be—that is what you would be officially told by a minister of the church when asked to explain why a prayer offered up in a deserving case has brought forth no response in kind.

Thy will be done on *earth, as it is in heaven.* Resident in the minds of so many people is the thought that God's will is nothing if not capricious. We cannot hope to know or understand His will, folk will say. Of course, they cannot, for they have made of it such an impossible thing. They have made of it a scapegoat, an explanation for something which seemingly cannot be explained upon any other grounds.

If they lose the physical presence of a dearly loved friend or relation through his transition in his early earthly life, then it is God's will that he should leave the earth-plane, God's will that he should suffer from some dreadful ailment that caused his passing. If people, or a whole nation, suffer a dire calamity, then it is God's will that it should be so.

So a lengthy chapter of disabilities, calamities, misfortunes, and disasters could be enumerated, all of which would be confidently attributed to the will of God. Would the same folk also ascribe to the will of God all the good things which they enjoyed? Would they say it is His will that they should enjoy a comfortable home in pleasant surroundings, enhanced by personal material prosperity?

Would they attribute a perfection of summer weather to His will, just as they alleged that it was His will that caused a hurricane of wind or a devastating earthquake? Most people are inclined to think that the will of God is distinctly one-sided, indulging in calamities rather than in benefits.

Who upon earth knows what is the will of God? Yet people pray for it to be done on earth *as it is in heaven* from which it must be assumed that they know what is God's will in heaven at least.

It is so easy in the presence of some inexplicable event or happening to place its cause in the will of God. It attaches blame in a case where personal suffering is undergone, but the word blame is very much softened if it is disguised beneath the words the *will of God*. How often is heard the cry in the midst of disaster: 'I suppose it is God's will, and I suppose there must be some reason for it, but I cannot understand it. Why should this happen to me?'

Not that such folk would assume some right of immunity from troubles of any kind, but because, so far, they had not encountered them: their lives had taken them along quietly upon an even course, untroubled by any major difficulties, but with an average proportion of minor difficulties that they were easily able to solve by their own ordinary endeavours. Then a greater tragedy overtakes them, apparently under the operation of the will of God, and they are nonplussed. The will of God has intruded into a happy and peaceful life, but for what sound reason it is impossible to understand.

Yet those unhappy souls may have earnestly prayed for years *Thy will be done* on *earth, as it is in heaven.*

And they would have assumed, presumably, that these apparent vagaries of will upon the part of God were the natural, everyday state of things in 'heaven' otherwise they would not have prayed for that particular exercise of divine will as they did. Would it not be wiser, then, to try to discover what is the will of God in heaven before praying for its extension to, and operation upon, earth?

That, it would be objected, is impossible. How can anyone know what is the will of God? Just so, and in that case were it not more expedient not to ask in prayer for something about which we can know nothing concerning its force or its power or its mode of operation, or, indeed, what consequences might follow a full response to the request?

Once again we see the remnants of paganism in all this confusion of ideas upon the will of God. In remote times, the same beliefs were held by man's ancestors upon earth in regard to his particular gods. These early gods were deities of very uncertain temper and temperament. They could smile or frown with equal faculty and with equal reason or lack of it—upon all people, regardless of their positions in life. At all costs the gods must be propitiated, because it was they who dispensed alike benefits and misfortunes upon all people.

It was their god's will that violent storms should sweep the countryside, that pestilences and plagues and famines should ravage the earth. They could never understand what it was impelled their gods to order such things, beyond the possibility, perhaps, that an insufficient number of sacrifices had been offered or that there had been a general want of respect and reverence. Where these reasons could not be adduced, then it was merely the will of their gods that it should be so.

When a multiplicity of gods were displaced in favour of one great God, these same absurd ideas were transferred to the Father of the universe. Orthodoxy has firmly retained them within the body of its teachings. and the people themselves have entertained the same beliefs that have been handed down from their pagan ancestors.

Again it may be countered: 'You are supposed to be living in a heaven of some sort; perhaps you could say, in broad terms, what is the will of God? The heaven you inhabit may not be the heaven of theology; it may not be the heaven that a great many people have envisaged as "paradise"—it may even be better than that; it may be a heaven, in the contemplation of which, many folk may be displeased or disturbed, or even revolted. Whichever it may be, your happiness seems to be of a high order, and it is a happiness which is enjoyed by millions of other people, so you claim. Can you not tell us something of the will of God?'

I can, but I can only tell you very little for the simple reason that there is really very little to tell! It is the earth people, led and inspired by orthodox teaching, who have made such an enormous factor of God's will.

I have said to you before, but I must say it again because, like so much that is extremely simple, the mere statement is apt to slip by almost unperceived, or with its full significance unrealised.

The will of the Father of the universe is that the whole universe of living things should be happy. The destiny of all mankind is ultimate supreme and unalloyed happiness which, in the spirit world, will one day be enjoyed by every single soul that is born upon earth. There lies before every person the whole of eternity of time in which to reach that sublime condition.

In the meantime, each soul will enjoy in the spirit

world a measure of felicity in exact keeping with his spiritual progression. When the feeling that the particular happiness is growing weak, is losing its edge, as it were, the moment has come for considering the means of taking another step forward upon the pathway of progression, and so bringing to the individual soul a fresh access of gratification.

Happiness. That is the supreme will of the Father of heaven and earth. Happiness, and everything that such happiness can connote. From that will of happiness comes the wish for the welfare of all mankind, whether incarnate or discarnate. The Father would never inflict one moment's sorrow upon any living soul. But what, it may be objected, of 'death' itself? Does not that alone bring sorrow and sadness to millions of people on earth?

Most assuredly it does, *but it need not; it was never intended that it should.* That is *not* God's will. Have we not already discussed the words *blessed are they that mourn, for they shall be comforted?* There would be no mourning upon earth if every man knew of the truths of the spirit world and of spirit life. If all men knew of and practised communication between our two worlds, and thus were enabled to speak with their departed friends and relatives and so continue a natural intercourse with them just as though they were still incarnate, if all men knew that truth, the sad tears that are so often shed would soon be wiped away to be shed no more.

No longer would it be conceived as the will of God that some tender flower of childhood should be taken from its happy home and family upon earth in the death of the physical body, to go, albeit, to greater happiness in the spirit world, but to leave behind deep sorrow and misery. For, however much one may rejoice that a cherished friend has gone to a higher life, there still remains the sadness of separation. But if, even in departure for the higher life, there remains no separation by virtue of the practice of communication, then there will be no sadness if the channels are provided for such communication.

The great misconception of ascribing so much to the will of God for which no other explanation can be found also arises from a misunderstanding of the causes of numberless things that take place upon earth. So much is put down to the will of God that is caused by none other than the will of man. So much is put down to the will of God that is nothing other than natural forces at work.

How many people for how many years believed that all diseases of the physical body were inflicted by God as a punishment? Numbers there are who believe it still. They will point to the New Testament, and quote Jesus as saying to one whom he had healed: *Thy sins are forgiven thee.* God had relented, forgiven the afflicted one his sins, and his disease had departed from him.

The storms and tempests that take place upon earth are not 'acts of God'. They are the work of natural forces. When certain conditions of atmosphere and temperature prevail, then meteorological disturbances ensue. They are *not* an intervention of the will of God.

When great wars are waged upon earth, it is not through the will of God that they take place, but through the will of man—of man alone. Wars are not 'sent' to the peoples of the earth world because they have misbehaved themselves in some wholesale fashion. From the Father of us all can come nothing that is not of the highest and best and purest, and war is of the lowest and worst and foulest. The Father, therefore, has no hand in it.

If one were to make a list of all the events, circumstances, and so forth, which are imputed solely to the will of God, the list would be a horrifying one. It would reveal in its cold narration not a Father of love, but a God whose mind would be anything but the perfect mind it is. It would reveal a Personage who could dispense with justice in favour of mercy, because of the applied merits of another's sacrifice, or through special pleading.

Thus there would be no true justice. It would reveal a Being of such uncertain and capricious mind that no human being would know when or where He would strike next. He might hammer out the life of any individual by inflicting upon him some dreadful disease, or He might send a great storm of wind and destruction, or a foul pestilence upon a whole nation; He might involve many nations in cruel and barbarous warfare where the slaughter is counted in hundreds of thousands of victims. The sins of the individual and of entire populations would be punished by direct intervention of God.

Thus you would be led to believe—and much more besides that is utterly erroneous—by those who are the properly constituted authority' for diffusing 'religious' teachings upon earth.

All this is so far, so dreadfully and deplorably far, from the truth concerning the personality of the Supreme Being. For no suffering of whatever nature or cause, no sadness or sorrow, no unhappiness, no afflictions of body or mind, no pestilences or diseases, no storms or great tempests upon land or sea, no famines, no wars, great or small, none of these visitations, as they are called, are caused, either directly or indirectly, by the Great Father of the universe.

All such terrestrial disasters appertain to the earth people and to them alone, and they have their causes either through the functioning of natural forces or through the evil ways of man upon earth. *They are not the will of God.* Nothing that is not for the good of mankind and for his happiness and welfare is according to the will of the Father. That, my good friend, is the one true and safe rule which you can apply to all events and circumstances that you will encounter during the term of an earthly life, and that condition of affairs has existed since the earth world became habitable. Seek always an earthly cause for all that is not manifestly for man's true happiness, and then you will begin to perceive something of the will of God.

Seeking forgiveness of God is perhaps one of the most general exhortations both embodied in prayers and included within the terms of formal statements of beliefs. 'The forgiveness of sins' committed against God—what are those 'sins'? I have no need to enumerate to you a long list of transgressions. I fancy they are sufficiently well known! But you are taught upon earth that when you commit sin you have offended God. I have told you, only a moment ago, how you cannot, you *simply cannot,* offend God.

Bethink you for one moment that if the Church's teaching were true, God would be existing in a continual and never-ending state of being offended because man is himself permanently in a state of sin. You have only to refer to the printed words of the various prayer-books to ascertain just what is man's spiritual condition—God is so immeasurably high, and poor mankind is so immeasurably low, a 'miserable sinner' in fact.

Forgive us our trespasses, as we forgive them that trespass against us. How many people can earnestly and sincerely and truthfully say, as they recite this part of the Lord's Prayer, that they have forgiven those who have trespassed against them? Assuredly such a sentence were better left unsaid. The latter half means little in the minds of so many people, and the first part can have no effect whatever upon any individual, however piously it may be said. and with whatever high hopes of receiving forgiveness the suppliant may have.

The Father cannot be offended. He has no forgiveness to give. He does not condemn; He does not punish, *nor does He relegate to others* either the power or the right to punish. The offences which the great majority of mankind commit are offences against natural laws, the laws that govern the spiritual nature of man, and those offences themselves react upon the one who commits them. We may offend fellowman, and we can—and we should—obtain his forgiveness. Then we can proceed to put ourselves in proper spiritual order.

In doing so, we shall have the help of the spirit world under the guidance of the Father of the universe Himself, through His ministers of the spirit world. We have not offended God; we have broken certain spiritual laws. If you were to cast yourself from a high wall in total disregard of the law of gravity you would have no one to blame but yourself because your physical body was drawn violently towards the ground at the cost of broken limbs or other injuries. In this respect you have 'broken' the law of gravity, but you have offended no one, injured no one, in this case, but yourself. The spiritual laws must be respected just as you upon earth respect the law of gravity, a law which is ever-present and so potent.

The dismal burden of so many of the 'authorised' prayers is the constant begging to God for mercy and the forgiveness of man's sins. This inveterate custom of hammering into the minds of the users of prayer-books their innate sinfulness is bad, for it sets up all manner of morbid conditions in the consciousness of folk with sensitive minds. The publicly recited prayers are no better in this respect. They forever proclaim man's sinfulness and unworthiness, until man himself, if he ponders upon the matter, can see very little hope in his future prospects when he passes into the spirit world. Mercy and forgiveness, these he will cling to, because he is taught that God is all merciful and will forgive the sins of all those who are truly contrite.

I have tried to explain to you how both mercy and forgiveness are not dispensed by the Father of Heaven. The Church will insist that it is right, and will so continue to stress these two points until it learns some degree of enlightenment. While the Church is spending so much time upon two erroneous beliefs it might be spending such valuable time in preaching and teaching the truth. Orthodoxy is blind, but its blindness does not merely affect the ecclesiastics who uphold it, it materially affects the thousands of souls who believe what those same ecclesiastics teach them.

Thus they arrive in the spirit world, when their earthly life is ended, with their minds clouded by ignorance and befogged by erroneous beliefs. We, in the spirit world, have to put this right. We have to bring knowledge of the truth to souls befuddled with earthly religious teachings which have woefully led them astray, not from the path of moral rectitude, but along the path of sheer ignorance of the conditions of life in spirit lands.

Speak to any one of such folk, and Orthodoxy would blush with shame could it hear the remarks that are made by these souls upon the way they have been misled. You can understand, then, how we have no great liking for the institutions which are responsible for this state of things. As it is, the errors of the Church have to be set right in the spirit world after countless souls have passed into it.

I have recounted to you the abject terror in which

numberless people arrive in these lands, actuated solely by the fear of the awful Judgement which is supposed to await every soul upon its transition. I have also recounted to you some details of the overwhelming relief which we are able to bring to these tortured souls. It is because I myself once taught such things that I now spend a great deal of my life in the spirit world coming to the instant rescue and relief of these spiritually deluded folk. Would that I had never given tongue to such errors when I was living on earth!

It is an uncomfortable feeling, I do assure you, to discover that what one taught with seeming authority has not a vestige of truth in it. It is more than uncomfortable; it is humiliating. But with complete understanding we can go to the aid of people who have themselves been afflicted by such teachings, and thus we can help to put things right not only for newly arrived friends in distress, but for ourselves as well.

There are too many 'mysteries' attached to the religions of the earth world, 'mysteries' which no one on earth or in the spirit world can solve or will ever be able to solve.

Religion is wrapped in strange problems, so many farfetched beliefs are held, so much time is wasted in the recital of incomprehensible creeds, that the whole business of travelling safely into the spirit world has become a hazardous process, something to be feared and dreaded, so problematical in its outcome, so circumscribed with pious nonsense which has no relation to the truth, so insulting to the Father of the universe, that man, by being constantly told that he is a 'miserable sinner' can only throw himself upon the mercy of God and beg forgiveness for his many 'sins'. Nothing could be more undignified than that man should grovel (as he is taught to do) in self-abasement under the overpowering weight of his supposed 'sins'.

It must not be supposed that I am suggesting that most of the inhabitants of the earth are saints. Very far from it. But the low spiritual degree in which most people have been placed by the alleged authority of earthly spiritual teachers is highly exaggerated. Mankind is not nearly so bad individually as the Churches would have him to be. The Church is no judge of such things. We in the spirit world are alone competent to appraise a man's *true* spiritual status. It is patent for all to see.

Let us forgive those who have offended us. That is vital, but let us not seek forgiveness from God. He does not give it because He has nothing to forgive. *He cannot be offended,* but we can break the laws of the spirit, and in breaking them we cannot ask the law to forgive us. But we can set about putting matters right so that we are again in harmony with that law and not defying it.

The Church teaches that no matter what 'sins' a person has committed, no matter how evil a life a man has led, God has infinite mercy and will forgive the truly contrite through the merits of the great soul whom the earth knows as Jesus.

Indeed, so immense are the powers accredited to Jesus, not only to achieve man's 'salvation' upon earth but in his advocacy at the High Court of Heaven that these suppositions form the termination of every 'official' prayer that is uttered publicly, or printed in the books for personal devotions. These peculiar terminations have seemed to take upon themselves a talismanic value, a magical power which most assuredly they do not, and cannot, possess.

As an article of prayer they are completely worthless. In fact, in any form or in any circumstances whatsoever, they are worthless. They are part of the huge theological edifice of spiritual error which the Church has erected and presented to the confusion of countless millions of souls when they ultimately arrive in the spirit world. They discover for themselves that it is useless to cry for mercy against the operation of a natural law which they have flouted and broken. They can cry aloud to the Father of Heaven, but not for mercy. That would be useless also.

But they can send forth then a prayer for help to the realms above them, and help will instantly be forthcoming, not in the shape of mercy nor in the form of forgiveness of 'sins', but some soul who is devoting his energies to those in distress will at once present himself—or herself—to the afflicted one. Thereupon the latter can disburden his troubled mind to his rescuer, who will be able to show him the means of redeeming the lost ground, not through the merits or sacrifice of another, but solely by his own endeavours.

Alone he must work out his own 'salvation', but with such actual assistance as to the ways and means of accomplishing it as, in his lack of knowledge, he will require. The recitation of a thousand creeds will avail him nothing. Faith of this description is valueless to advance the soul one fraction of an inch upon the way of progression.

Our best friend, in such cases, can only offer and give friendly assistance; the actual work of personal 'redemption' is carried out by the individual concerned *alone*. He it is who must set about putting himself in harmony with the laws he has broken, however they may have been broken, and to whatever extent. If his offences are against others, his first act will be to seek the forgiveness of those whom he has wronged.

The latter will readily forgive him for you must know that enmities can quickly cease in the spirit world in certain quarters. Then he will be quickly shown how to redeem himself to fit himself for taking up his undoubted heritage of happiness in these lands. His past errors will have been set right by his own endeavours and not by any magical process of vicarious atonement: by personal application, possibly by sheer hard work.

The Church which makes such boastful claims upon earth has contributed nothing in truth or knowledge or assistance towards helping the soul in its life in the spirit world. The very prayers which are said for the 'dead' are based upon knowledge so faulty that they are of little or no help to the 'departed' soul. The Church has, in fact, disastrously failed. And the failure of the Church is for all to see here in these spirit lands where we have to set right the effect upon the 'faithful' of its multitudinous errors.

Perhaps one of the gravest misconceptions of the Father of the universe is expressed in the last words of this prayer we are discussing: *Lead us not into temptation.* Here again we are not concerned with the original documents of the New Testament, but solely with the words as I have here set them down and as they are also set down in the myriad printed copies of the gospels. The theologian will object that no sane person would ever believe God Himself would deliberately lead a single human being into temptation, but there are many, many sane people who *do* believe it, who, moreover, believe every word of the New Testament *exactly as it is recorded* in their own language, people who would disagree with the theologian most emphatically.

God, they would affirm, *does* most certainly lead us into temptation, and if we fail in spiritual strength and fall into 'sin', and 'die unrepentant', then we shall be damned for all eternity. Then would follow the usual crude and nonsensical beliefs held by such people.

The theologian in this instance would be right—God would not, does not, *cannot,* lead a single individual into temptation. But why voice the wicked suggestion that He does? Why, above all things, say one thing and mean exactly the opposite? Thus do words lose their meaning entirely. Such verbal methods would never be tolerated for an instant in the ordinary intercourse of daily life upon the earth-plane—or upon any other plane of existence.

Chaos would result inevitably if we persisted in saying one thing while, at the same time, meaning something entirely the opposite. Precision and exactitude in important, as well as in the lesser, matters of daily life, would be for ever lacking, or, at least, one would never know if words were to be taken as they stand, or if the reverse meaning were intended. Ordinary affairs could never be carried on if verbal conditions of that sort prevailed. Yet such rhetorical looseness of words and speech is freely tolerated in so vitally important a subject as prayer.

If there is one thing where precision and exactitude is essential it is in the framing of prayer. We have already discussed that aspect of the matter, and I have given you some suggestions upon the subject. Here I will amplify what I have given you by emphasising the fact that theological theories which are incorporated within so many prayers are perfectly useless and completely ineffective. They are so many empty words, and as such would be far better omitted altogether. They merely serve to confuse the main purport of the prayer.

The recitation of religious beliefs during the course of praying are equally worthless, whether those beliefs are true beliefs or just the recital of fallacious doctrines, and again but serve to confuse the real purport of the prayer. There is no spiritual value whatever in affirming, either publicly or privately, one's religious beliefs in the form of a set and recognised creed, or in a creed of one's own composition.

In the ages past it became the custom of congregations to make these public avowals as a means of demonstrating clearly that they were of the true faith and not contaminated by the heretical beliefs of others. Such ostentatious displays had no more spiritual value then as now.

To return to the Lord's Prayer. Though the churchman would strenuously deny that God would ever lead man into temptation, despite the statement to the contrary in the Lord's Prayer, yet the same ecclesiastic would assert that God will 'try' a person; that is, tribulations will be 'sent' to him to test the quality of his spiritual power of resistance, and though, properly speaking, temptation comes from 'the devil', yet God *allows* 'the devil' to do his fell work—and so on, upon the same lines.

Indeed, when one comes to weigh these things up, the God of theology has laid so many traps for the unheeding, has made life upon earth, in its relation to life in the spirit world, such a mass of complexities of dogma, and made 'heaven' into such a pious, almost impossible place, that many an individual is fully justified in shuddering at the prospect of going there. He will associate the 'hereafter' with the particular brand of religion which he favoured or with which he was most familiar, and if he allows himself to think at all upon the matter he will compare the life he is now living, which may be comfortable enough to suit his desires, With the 'religious' type of life that is associated in his mind with the Church's 'heaven'.

He will feel that, at least as far as he is concerned, he will be something of a fish out of water, and living in a constant state of embarrassment among people of a degree of piety to which he could never hope to attain. This confusion in the minds of men has not arisen solely through the Church's erroneous teaching, but it has also been brought about by the very contents of official prayers.

If a person is a churchgoer he will regularly hear the words *lead us not into temptation* addressed to the Father. What is the result? If he believes that God may at any moment lead him to temptation by acting as that extremely unpleasant functionary, an *agent provocateur,* he is doing himself no spiritual good by believing such a mischievous thing. If he does *not* believe that the Father would ever tempt him to transgress, then by saying directly the opposite in his prayer, he is failing in the first principle of successful prayer, namely, that a prayer should be clear and exact in its terms and thoughts.

So many people say their prayers faithfully and earnestly, but alas, they will tell you that they never seem to be answered. There may be many reasons for that. I shall hope to go into some of them with you presently. For the moment, however, objections may be raised as to what I have said concerning the Lord's Prayer, the most widely cherished and favourite among prayers.

'Who is this fellow,' it may be objected, 'who tries to demolish the actual prayer that was given to the world by Jesus himself as a model for all prayers?'

I would answer that this prayer has never been used as a model for all prayers, as it is plain to see by the fulsome compositions which are daily recited, and which appear in the prayer-books. The precedent—whether fortuitously implied, or not—the precedent of precision and succinctness has been totally ignored in favour of oratorical exhibitions framed in lengthy periods and pompous phraseology.

As to the prayer having been given to the world by Jesus, as I observed at the outset, whoever was the author of it, it certainly was *not* Jesus. His spiritual knowledge was in those times far too great for him to have fallen into any such error.

Prayer Answered

There is another aspect of prayer to which we could profitably devote some attention, and it might it expressed thus: is prayer answered? That is a question which exercises a great many minds upon earth.

Some will assert most emphatically that prayer is answered, and they will bring forward a personal experience to demonstrate their claim. Others, not so fortunate, will deny that prayer is answered because they have had no personal experience of it. From this opposed evidence, the incarnate might answer our initial question in this manner: prayer is *sometimes* answered, but it depends entirely upon the will of God.

If our supplication is in accordance with God's will, we shall have our request granted: if it is against God's will, we shall not. If only we could obtain some glimmering (the incarnate might add) of what is God's will, then we should have a solution to the whole problem of the efficacy of prayer.

Once again we have the introduction of the will of God to provide an explanation for a spiritual state of affairs where seemingly no other explanation can be found—this time to explain the failure or otherwise of prayer. So unsatisfactory is this reason that the will of God becomes translated into the whim of God for upon no other grounds can be based the apparent partiality and capriciousness in God's exercising of His will, and the general uncertainty of prayers being answered.

The experience of most people is that they pray to the Father for some especial purpose while at the same time they are completely uncertain in their minds of what the issue will be—if any. It may mean success, or it may mean failure. Even if it be alleged that any cause of failure must be attributed to lack of faith, the suppliant may retort that he reposed absolute faith in his prayer being answered. Nothing, indeed, could appear to be more hazardous than the outcome of prayer where some particular request is made.

Many a pious soul will hide his disappointment and sadness, resulting from the failure of his prayer, in the words *Thy will be done.* And with that despairing cry all hopes have finally vanished for to whom can he now appeal? For some inscrutable reason God has not seen fit, he would say, to answer his prayer, and so there is nothing more that can be done.

In the spirit world, we never make use of the words *Thy will be done.* We prefer to say, in effect, *Thy wisdom prevail.* And God's wisdom prevails. It prevails in every single instance—*without fail.* That wisdom is manifested through the illustrious personages who inhabit the highest realms, and to whom we turn in whatever major difficulties we may have. When we have any request to make, we find the answer comes to us instantly, whether it be yes or no. But that does not come within our present consideration since you are not yet an inhabitant of these lands.

Let us rule out, forever, any notion that the will of God is concerned with the answering of your prayers, and if we discuss *how* they are answered we shall see at once why it is that on occasion they are not answered.

We are, of course, only considering prayers that contain a specific request, whether it be for spiritual guidance in some form or other, or whether it be for material assistance during time of difficulty or distress. With prayers of thanksgiving, or with the many pious ejaculations that appear in the prayer-books, we are not here concerned.

It is widely supposed that God, being omnipotent and omniscient, responds to the prayers of the incarnate Himself. If a fully answered prayer is connected with any matter concerning the Church, the whole occurrence is regarded as a 'miracle', or the next thing to it. In such a case, though, it may not be due to the *direct* intervention of God. The answer to the prayer may be alleged to have come about through the kind offices of some 'saint' of the Church. It is because of the belief that prayers are answered through the direct intervention of God that so much misapprehension exists.

Miracles do not happen. Nothing happens upon earth—or in the spirit realms—that is above or beyond natural laws. There is no such thing or state as that of being 'supernatural'.

How certain minds upon earth love to refer to anything touching upon the spirit world as 'supernatural'! From the supposed vision in the sky to the haunting of a house, all alike are 'supernatural'; the ghosts and the goblins and the apparitions, with a variety of other choice designations, all are used to indicate a dweller in spirit lands.

To those who use such words in offensive ridicule or in pure thoughtlessness, I would say: have a care. Remember that every soul who lived on earth now lives in the spirit world, among whom must be numbered your own good friends and relations who have passed on. Unless you would claim for them the spiritual altitude of 'saints', then they are living upon slightly lower planes, and they must be counted among the many millions of us here. Be cautious of using such a term to describe a spirit person as may, in time, be used against you in similar offensive derision.

This very mundane view of the spirit world is held by the incarnate because they consider themselves in most respects as superior to the inhabitant of the spirit world by virtue of the fact that the incarnate are still upon earth, the good, firm earth where reality surrounds them. They are living the normal life. In the spirit world it is vastly different. *That* is vague and shadowy, unseen and far off; the denizens of those regions are ghosts, spectres, or wraiths; shadows, in fact, the very land they live in must be unsubstantial because, like its inhabitants, it cannot be seen with the eye in the healthy fashion in which things can be perceived upon the substantial earth.

The spirit world, to these minds, is an unhealthy place altogether, and the less said about it—or even thought about it—the better. There are many people who think this way, and who are still living upon earth. There are millions of people in the spirit world who thought that way themselves, once upon a time, when they were incarnate. They all experienced a shock to their self-satisfaction when they discovered the truth of things for themselves upon their arrival in these lands. However, this is something of a digression, I am afraid. Let us resume.

If we examine the procedure of the answering of prayer we shall be able to see why prayer at times is not answered.

First of all, a supplication is made to the Father. It is impossible for me to go into the details of every type of petition for reasons which you will readily understand. There are millions upon millions of requests coming into the spirit world, and each with enormously differing intentions, conditions and circumstances. Every prayer is taken care of, individually. If the thoughts have been fully concentrated upon the words or the intention which the words clothe, and if it has adequate directive power behind it, then that prayer will unfailingly reach its high destination.

For our present purposes we will consider that the prayer has reached those realms of light. Our first point of contact with it will be, thenceforward, with the spirit guide of the person who sent forth the prayer.

Here I must explain that every human being upon earth is in the spiritual charge of a wise and experienced soul who is known technically upon the earth-plane as a spirit guide. Spirit guides belong to a noble order of beings in the spirit world. They have all been resident in these lands for many hundreds of years, and they are especially chosen for their work because of the high degree of wisdom which they possess among their many other important attributes. The guides have charge of their wards from the latters' infancy. They are, therefore, fully conversant with all the circumstances and affairs in the lives of their charges. Happiest are those among the incarnate who, while yet upon earth, have met their spirit guides and spoken with them.

Your spirit guide is fully conversant with whatever prayers you may say which contain a request. The guide, being familiar with the content of certain of your prayers, it is but natural that he should undertake the task—often an extremely difficult one—of bringing about an answer to them.

But the guide does not essay this task alone; he will have a number of willing helpers. In many cases they will be either the friends or relations of the suppliant or both. Those friends or relations may either be resident in the spirit world, or some may still be upon the earth-plane. The actual process, then, of answering a prayer consists in influencing, impressionally or inspirationally, such persons upon earth as are in a position to bring about the fulfilment of the suppliant's wishes, either directly or indirectly.

The spirit guide will in every case use his judgement and discretion as to whether a prayer shall be answered fully and at the earliest possible moment, whether it shall be answered only partially or conditionally where such is practicable; whether the prayer shall be remitted to some future time when conditions and circumstances are more propitious. Finally, the guide will exercise his discretion as to whether the wishes of the suppliant shall be fulfilled at all.

The guide's wisdom will tell him that for some wish to be granted to his charge would prove harmful to the latter, physically or spiritually or materially. In such case no action whatever would be taken, nor would it be permitted, and the prayer will remain unanswered.

Naturally, it is not all requests which, in their fulfilment, are injurious to the person who makes the supplication, but the fulfilment might be injurious to others, and therefore, it will not be granted.

Here let it be said that more prayers, by countless thousands, are answered completely and fully than are left unanswered. If it be wise and possible and practicable, a prayerful request will be granted without doubt. The will of God does not enter into the matter, but most decidedly the *wisdom* of God does. That wisdom is manifested through the spirit guides of the incarnate, and it is derived, where necessary, from the highest beings. But it must be remembered that spirit guides do not possess almighty powers, although they draw their power from the Father Himself.

When a spirit guide commences to set in motion the various forces to influence, by impression, certain people upon earth, he will always be cognizant of the percipients' free will. He is bound to respect it, and to do nothing that will in any way infringe the right of exercising it.

Thus far I have but treated the subject in the abstract. Let me give an example which will, I hope, serve to clarify the matter; such an example as we might choose from scores upon scores. The variety of requests that are contained in prayers is endless, as you can imagine when you consider for a moment the vast diversification of human affairs and circumstances that constitute the lives of people still living upon the earth.

Everyone has his particular wants and ambitions, and although countless numbers of people never give a thought to prayer in this connection, yet there are still countless numbers who do. Here, then, is a simple example, and a common one.

A son or daughter—shall we say?—prays fervently that the mother, who is dangerously ill, may not be 'taken from them in death'. The prayers, however, are unavailing, and the mother 'dies'. Why was this particular request seemingly refused when so much happiness would have ensued if had been granted in the mother's recovery?

The religiously inclined, as well as Orthodoxy itself, would reply that it was not the will of God that the lady should remain upon earth, that God 'called' her to another life, and so on, all of which is very far from the mark. Let us see what happened, or could happen, when that prayer was sent out.

Before—perhaps long before—any prayers for the lady's recovery were ever uttered, the spirit guide of the mother was already in as close attendance upon her as possible with spirit doctors. The prayer in this event would not be lost or redundant, but would serve to bring them all, the patient, the guide, and the doctors, in much closer rapport, and so, if it were possible to effect a cure, that cure would most certainly be brought about.

On the other hand, the patient might have been so far removed in attunement with her spirit guide that he would have been unable to draw sufficiently close because of the material barrier separating them, a barrier that was erected by the patient's material thoughts, or her mode of life, or her heedlessness of anything beyond the earthly plane of existence, or from a variety of other causes.

The prayer might help to disperse this eventually, but by then it might be too late for the disease might have gained far too great a hold to respond to treatment from either world, yours or ours. The result, therefore, is inevitable, and a transition takes place. But the transition will have taken place in spite of help that was actually given from the spirit world, and not because help was withheld.

So you see, here we have what appears, from a earthly point of view, a clear case of the failure of prayer. But the prayer itself has not failed inasmuch as it was fully answered to the best ability of all those who were concerned in its answering. The true failure was not upon the part of the prayer or upon the part of those who were undertaking its answer. In this particular instance—as in thousands of others—the fault lies with the incarnate.

The powers of spirit healers or doctors are not infallible or omnipotent. In all cases they will work to the utmost of their capabilities to prolong the earthly span of any incarnate person under their care, but they cannot prolong life in any person upon earth indefinitely. The tissues will themselves wear out in the natural course of things, and transition takes place.

There are many people still living upon earth who owe their continued life upon that plane to the spirit doctors and their self-sacrificing earthly instruments. Such people may be fully aware of the fact, and they are highly appreciative of what has been done. There are many more who could have the enormous advantages of this service, but they do not believe such a thing possible, or they find the whole subject distasteful. Again, there are others who pray for their recovery, and expect that, by the *direct* intervention of God, they will be made whole again. But they make no forthright effort to help the unseen spirit folk who are doing their utmost to restore the patient to a state of sound health.

So one could go on multiplying not only different cases, but an immensity of different circumstances. What so many people do not realise is that the simplest request contained in a prayer may mean an enormous amount of work upon the part of the spirit people concerned in bringing about the suppliant's wishes. Again, what so many do not grasp is that when prayers contain a specific request of a material nature, the fulfilment of the prayer must in the ultimate devolve upon some *person or persons who are still incarnate.* And it does not stop there. The more susceptible an incarnate person is to the impressions which come from the spirit world, so much the greater are the chances of a successful issue to a prayer.

It is very easy to say a simple little prayer containing some request but to bring an answer may involve the influencing of any number of people on earth, including the person who has said the prayer. It may be necessary to lead the latter carefully in the right direction, to impress him to get into contact with certain people who, in turn, will get into contact with others, and so forming as complete a chain of individuals as is possible to imagine so that in the end the right person may be reached, and the prayer fully answered.

It may rest—indeed, it so often does rest—with our

ability to impinge our thoughts upon the last person with sufficient vigour to achieve our purpose and the purpose of the prayer. The whole structure of human contacts may be demolished by the inability of the last individual to receive our direct impressions. We may then have to retrace our steps, as it were, and endeavour to find another who is less material in mind and outlook, or whose psychic faculties are keener, and so construct another chain of persons, another group of links.

No, my good friend, the answering of prayer is not child's play. It not infrequently involves a vast deal of hard work upon our part.

Sometimes we are able to interview people when they come to visit these lands during their sleep state, and lay our case before them. Seldom do we have a refusal to our wishes on behalf of our friend in need upon earth. Such people are most times eager and ready to help us by falling in with our wishes—while they are upon their nocturnal or other sleep-state visit. Their intentions are pure and genuine and honest, but, alas, when they return to their earthly bodies and recover their physical consciousness, it so often happens that they take with them no recollection whatever of their good intentions and resolutions to do what we desire of them. But we persevere, and keep on persevering, until either we achieve success, or until we are obliged reluctantly to abandon our efforts altogether, or at least for some more auspicious time and occasion.

The principal trouble beneath which prayer has so long laboured comes from the wrong views which people on earth hold in respect of it. For many, many years, the incarnate have expected *too much* of prayer. For so long Orthodoxy has dinned into the ears of its 'faithful' that prayer is practically all-powerful. It is no such thing. God will answer your prayers, it is asserted, if it be His will to do so or if you have sufficient faith—or both. Thus, is prayer bolstered up and kept alive, while any failures are imputed to God's will or lack of faith.

Faith in what, or whom? You will be able to perceive for yourself just how much has faith to do with the answering of prayer. People can have absolute faith, as they allege, but the prayer is still unsuccessful. A strong, firm, good intention is by far the best. Faith is too unsubstantial, too vague. But a firm resolve to help the prayer to the utmost of one's abilities upon earth, to be as cheerful as circumstances will allow, to be hopeful, and to be confident and sure that, provided the request in the prayer will harm no one, including the suppliant, then a great array of spirit helpers and friends will labour unremittingly to fulfil the wishes expressed in the prayer. It requires no faith.

It will be seen that the over-expectation of the results of prayer, together with the faulty conception of the means used to answer it, are responsible for a great deal of public prayer that is completely useless. Such, for example, as public prayers for rain, or for any other changes in meteorological conditions. How could we possibly alter the weather from the spirit world? We cannot do so any more than can you upon earth alter it.

The spirit world has no influence whatever over the states of the weather on earth. The changes in the weather are brought about by the natural laws which govern the atmosphere of the material world. Alteration of atmosphere and temperature produce their varying results, but they cannot be influenced by anyone from the spirit world as is sometimes supposed. It has even been suggested that the earthly elements are under the particular supervision of some great soul in spirit lands. That is impossible.

If Orthodoxy only knew the truth about prayer. Its efficacy, its *limitations,* and the *modus operandi* of answering it, it would never in the past have made prayer ridiculous with such exhibitions as 'prayers for rain'. Orthodoxy is no more enlightened now upon the subject, and still clings to the will of God to provide an explanation for something—indeed many things—which it is at a complete loss to understand, but which may be found in the simple exposition of a spiritual truth or the operation of a spiritual law. Orthodoxy has not even yet learned how to pray. How can it instruct others when its own ignorance and lack of knowledge is so profound?

Baptism

The laws of the spirit world are the visible contradiction of a vast deal of theology, of so many man-made doctrines, creeds, and dogmas, and of so large a part of the *impedimenta* that go to make up Orthodox religion.

One of my very early discoveries here was that one law of the spirit world, just one law, can completely falsify perhaps three or four doctrinal beliefs of the earth world.

One can perceive, as a resident of the spirit world, that the earthly Church has, in its own estimation, practically taken command of the spirit world. The Church has, in effect, built a code of complicated laws by which the soul of mortal man should be governed. It has elevated the earth to a position of far wider importance than in truth it warrants.

The earth world is of some importance in the evolution of the soul of man, and it naturally takes its place in the full scheme of existence. But the earth is merely a steppingstone to a higher life, the higher life of the spirit world. The 'religious' life of man upon the earth-plane should be as free as the air that he breathes. The Church has no right, no mandate, to circumscribe any soul with cramping man-made beliefs that have no approximation whatever to the truth, and that are a hindrance and not a help to man's spiritual progression.

The Church has formulated doctrines whereby the soul's exact state and place of abode in the spirit world have been pre-assigned to him. It has made laws, the breaking of which by man will inevitably consign him to hell for all eternity. It performs rites which, in point of absolute fact, are entirely useless to any soul, and which will not help that soul one step of the way upon his journey into the spirit world, or after.

A great deal of weight has been attached to the opinions and statements of the very early churchmen, whose so-called learning has elevated them to the title of Fathers of the Church. Never did fathers lead their children so woefully astray. They were for the most part as much in the dark as those whom they were professing to instruct. Those same Fathers of the Church are all of them in this world of spirit.

A host of them are great souls, but their views are vastly different now from those they held when upon earth. It was the contention of one of these Fathers when he was incarnate that in whatever spiritual state a man's soul might be when his 'death' took place, in that state would it always remain. As the tree falls, so will it lie. The moment that 'death' took place, then, a man's spiritual future was sealed. If he had misbehaved himself when upon earth, then hell was to be his portion, or perhaps, with better fortune, a sojourn of unspecified duration in purgatory. During his short life upon earth, therefore, a man would determine his abode in the spirit world for all eternity. It is upon such dicta as this that so much of Church doctrine has been founded.

In the spirit world, we are faced with reality, faced with the truth beyond all equivocation. As a priest of the Church, I performed numerous ceremonies. Since my coming to the spirit world I have seen the truth and the worth of such rites. My mind has been cleared—just as the minds of millions of others here have also been cleared—of all the falsity of so much of the religious teachings of the earth. In speaking to you thus, therefore, I give you the truth as it is known to us all in these realms.

You are not living in a world where the truth is ever to be beheld. We are, if I were to temper my statements by tampering with the truth, of what use for me to speak at all?

Such communications from the spirit world would be utterly valueless. In matters appertaining to the soul and the future spiritual status of man, such an attitude would make the earth world always right and the spirit world always wrong. That is a position which we in the spirit world cannot accept. The spirit world cannot and will not take its orders from the earth world.

The Church leaders know practically nothing about the 'future state'. They should do. Instead, they uphold and diffuse preposterous doctrines which are alleged to have a Divine origin and source. In most cases these doctrines are pure trivialities which a few moments of life here in the spirit world will reveal as having evolved from trivial minds. With my fuller experience of the spirit world, I have sometimes shuddered in recalling how some petty doctrine is inseparably associated with the Greatest Mind of the universe.

When I was on earth, I fully believed that to 'die' unbaptised was to be deprived of entry to the realms of heaven. The greatest extreme of all was to believe that unbaptised persons who passed to the spirit world in that condition were condemned to hell for ever. I therefore regarded the whole ceremony of baptism as of the utmost importance to the soul's 'salvation'. I deemed it, in fact, indispensable. I believed that it completely washed away every trace of 'sin' if the baptism were performed upon one who had already reached the 'age of reason'.

I believed that were a person to omit being baptised

until he was upon his death-bed, that being then baptised he would go straight to heaven. And further, that whatever misdeeds he had committed, those misdeeds would be taken from him in the twinkling of an eye, that his soul would be spotless and fit only for the highest heaven. I did not know then, as I know now, that there is no mystic or magic formula that will eradicate from an evil-doer the results of his evil ways. It was part of my faith that as, and when, I baptised an infant so I saved that infant for the realms of heaven; that had that infant 'died' without the performance of this ceremony, or at least without the barest recital even by a layman of the few brief but essential words of the actual baptism, that child would be forever deprived of the sight of God. He would never be able to see God 'face to face'.

It did not occur to me, as I now know to be the case, that the spiritual beauty of the infant's soul was itself a part of the Father of Heaven Himself, and that no words uttered by any person upon the earth-plane could add one trace more beauty to that soul. The soul that is implanted within the child is perfect.

There is one law, at least, in the spirit world that entirely opposes the rite of baptism, and that is the law of cause and effect.

It is a bad doctrine this baptismal 'washing away of sins'. Many are the souls we have met here who were shocked to learn that scores of happy children who live in the children's realm have passed into the spirit world unbaptised. When they came to understand their new situation and the laws that govern this world, they soon realised that the spirit law that brings all the children from the earth world into their own realm in the spirit world is far, far greater than any baptismal rite. Indeed, it becomes trifling beside the truth and beauty of the children's sphere.

To retain the rite purely as a traditional symbol, as it were, of dedicating the infant to God, would be harmless, since it would involve no one in the belief of any obscure doctrines. To perform some simple ceremony of naming an infant, and at the same time to offer thanks for having emerged safely from the ordeal of child-birth, that, too, is harmless. But to go beyond this is unquestionably wrong.

It will be remarked, perhaps, that the Scriptures, upon which so much of the Christian religion is founded, clearly state that we must be baptised, and that even the words of the formula are given, without the exact recital of which the whole ceremony is void. That is so. But because this appears in the Scriptures. I cannot alter the laws of the spirit world were I even willing and able to do so—and most emphatically I am not so! The spirit world and the laws of the spirit world are a great deal more important than some words that are alleged to have been spoken nearly two thousand years ago.

The spurious importance that has been attached to the rite of baptism is but another instance of the false position in which Christianity has been placed, giving it an exclusiveness to which it has no right. That exclusiveness has been extended until it not only reaches far out into the spirit world, but until it almost encroaches upon the Father of the universe Himself. If Christian Orthodoxy has not entirely claimed the full possessive rights of approach to the Father of the universe, it certainly claims the most extensive privileges for all who call themselves Christians, whether good or bad.

Is it in the spirit of true justice that some should be more privileged than others in matters of their 'soul's salvation'? Many will answer yes, because they consider that the Christian religion is above and beyond all others simply because it is 'Christian'. That is not a satisfactory reason, but it is one that, nevertheless, is most commonly given. When we come to discuss things with people here we find that they staunchly upheld their Christianity when upon earth, but can give no adequate reason why they did so. Some will assert that they were baptised into the Christian religion at birth, and so they have called themselves Christians ever since.

They naturally assume—at first—that they are in a Christian heaven, a heaven that is the reward for being a good Christian—or at least for being a Christian at all—and of leading a good life. And in the course of time their eyes are opened. When they set out, as I did, upon a voyage of discovery through these realms, they begin meet people who, to say the very least, cannot really *belong* to these *Christian* realms in which they fondly imagine they are now living. They will see visitors from the higher realms whose very cast of countenance would suggest that they were not Christians; the colour of their skin and their general appearance, too, will add to this rather surprising discovery.

None of these souls was ever baptised, and so, according to some beliefs, they should have been 'cast into exterior darkness'. Certainly, they would seem to have no business to be dwelling in these realms. But the stubborn fact remains that they *are* dwelling in these realms, and they are here regardless of race, or colour, or creed.

The three distinctions have no validity, no significance whatever in the spirit world. Race and colour form no hindrance to the soul's grand progressional march, and those of us who ever entertained narrow and insular views upon the matter are compelled by force of the truth to readjust our views. Those of us who, when incarnate, preferred to regard people of other races and nationalities as human beings like ourselves, find that when we meet such people in the spirit world they are our friends, glad to know us as we are happy to know them. The colour of the skin and the contour of the nose are matters upon which we have no thought at all.

In these realms we are a great company of true friends, as proud to know one whose countenance is dusky as we are to know one whose features are pale by comparison.

Gone for ever are racial prejudices and the feelings of estrangement between men of different racial colour. Amongst all this immense population of various nationalities there are millions who were not baptised when they were upon earth, millions who acknowledged allegiance to no religion, but who lived their lives according to their conscience, and who behaved towards their neighbour as they would have their neighbour behave towards them. They were unhampered by any form of religious creed when they finally arrived in the spirit world.

I have said that people are here in these realms regardless of creed. By that I mean that whatever creed such people professed when they were incarnate has made no difference to their *abode* in the spirit world. They have earned their abode by the kind of life they led upon the earth-plane, and by that means alone. But their religious beliefs usually undergo a vast reconstruction after their transition has taken place, when they find that Orthodoxy has been peremptorily halted at the very portals of the spirit world. The churches that exist here in the old earthly form are mere religious pretenders and of no significance whatever.

In the light of our new experiences in the spirit world, we can see just what degree of reliance can be placed upon tradition in the ordering of the religious side of life upon earth. We can see how nation after nation for generation after generation has held on to the belief of the vital necessity of the baptismal rite as the spiritual key that will unlock the doors of the spirit world to the arriving soul.

We can see that Orthodoxy regards the unbaptised person as standing in deadly peril of the loss of 'salvation' of his soul. Many incarnate people treat such a person as a spiritual outcast, doomed to eternal perdition, fit only for the lowest hell. Orthodoxy is blindly ignorant and unwilling to learn. Throughout the centuries past it has built up an elaborate system of religious observances and religious teachings which are in the main completely worthless. The Churches have arrogated to themselves powers over the individual soul which have no basis in truth or fact. Indeed, these powers are nothing but a sham; they can never be substantiated. The Church can boast, it can try to circumscribe a soul with threats of spiritual disaster if it disobeys its counterfeit 'commandments'.

It can try to impose all manner of restricting conditions upon its members; it can all but stifle the spiritual life out of man; it can live its self-satisfied, genteel life upon the earth-plane, proudly proclaiming, in its presumptuous way, what it fondly believes to be the 'will of God'.

It can go upon its superior way condemning men, on the one hand, to everlasting fire and, upon the other, converting them into 'saints' of the Church. The Church can go on doing these absurd things, while we in the spirit world assess them at their true valuation. And it falls upon us in the spirit world to try to counteract all fallacious teachings that have been imbibed by the Church's deluded adherents when they ultimately arrive in the spirit world.

Have I not told you how, in company with others, I am engaged upon the work of helping people immediately after they have left the earth world? We try to show them that all is well, and that splendid happiness awaits them, here and now, if they will but forget the stupid teachings of their earthly Church, cast fear from their minds, and look about them at the glories and wonders of their new land.

We and many others are continually engaged upon this work, and it is made supremely necessary by the blind religious teachings of the earth world. Never, for one moment, do we begrudge an instant of the time we devote to this work, but what I do now, in the name of us all and with the utmost vigour, is to protest against the state of affairs that should bring this work about, namely, to put right in the spirit world the results of the abysmal religious blunders of the earth world.

It is a humiliating discovery to find, after we have arrived in the spirit world, that not only are most of our religious ideas wrong, but also that we have spent our time, as part of our life's work on earth, in passing on those erroneous ideas to other people. Did I say humiliating? It is much more—it is absolutely crushing! Is it to be wondered at, therefore, that we hasten to set right, at the very first opportunity, the false teachings that we have disseminated while on earth, by helping those who, as a result of such teaching, have arrived here spiritually bemused.

The earth world is existing in a state of spiritual fog. The mists of Orthodox teachings have settled upon Christians and blotted from their sight every glimpse of the spirit world, a world that in reality is so near to them, but which Orthodoxy has made so remote. The teachers in the Churches are floundering in a morass of spiritual ignorance. When they arrive here, the weight of that ignorance presses down upon them in its full force. Their eyes are soon opened however—opened for the first time.

They find that the jargon that stood them in such good stead and covered a wealth of spiritual ignorance is no longer of any value. The very words have an empty sound now. In one second of time, almost, they see practically the whole of their beliefs tumbling in ruins about them. All their most cherished doctrines are swept away by the plain fact of their being in the spirit world and faced with the truth. They see their theology reduced to its proper dimensions. They see that from a grain of truth there has grown a great false creed, perhaps, or that from some simple and natural act there has been built up a huge edifice of ritualistic performance, attendance at which the laity will avoid only upon deadly peril to their 'immortal souls'.

These ministers of the Church will see that some doctrine or another to which they so steadfastly clung has now become mere nonsense, to be quickly cast aside as useless. They will discover that their dogmas and creeds have paled into complete insignificance in the light of the great truths that are confronting them upon every hand in the spirit world. They will regret the time they have spent upon earth in supporting such untruth.

Some of these people are wrathful that they should have lived in such ignorance, wrathful that others should have so led them astray. Others are wrathful with themselves for not seeing what is now so perfectly obvious to them. They feel humiliated that, after studying so much, the 'knowledge' which they gained is not knowledge at all.

They feel humiliated that they took upon themselves so much authority over the spiritual lives of other people. They feel humiliated in the remembrance of what they taught and preached, and of the feelings of superiority and spiritual security that their positions gave them. They feel humbled when they recall the number of times they spoke so freely of the 'will of God' to cover up the deficiencies of their teachings, or to soothe some soul in distress. They will recall the long and fulsome prayers which they felt were the only kind acceptable to the Supreme Being.

They will shiver at the very thought of how they regarded themselves as being looked upon with especial favour by the Deity because they had been called to their high and holy office of minister of the Church. When the full and crushing realisation of all this comes upon them, they seek to hide themselves away that they may recover from the state of overwhelming mortification which such revelations have brought upon them. They will eventually emerge from their self-communion, strengthened by the truth as they now know it, and they will solicit that help which is ever at the command of us here in every realm and region of the spirit world.

And how do I know all this? Why, my dear friend, I know it because I have witnessed it many, many times in my work among priests of my own former Church as well as among those of other communities. It is most absorbing work, and it has brought us a host of grand and enthusiastic friends. We labour together to bring solace to souls in distress, as we were once similarly distressed ourselves. So it will ever go on until the earth world becomes more enlightened and the incarnate pass to us here with a full knowledge of what is before them. It will be a happy day when that happens—and many of us will have to cast about for something else to do!

If I thus demolish the 'sacred' rite of baptism, it may be asked, what becomes of the words of Jesus containing his injunction to 'go ye therefore, and teach all nations, baptising them in the name of the Father, and of the Son, and of the Holy Ghost'? Why, they just recede into their proper place, or to be more exact, they reveal their true value. Jesus never spoke those words. He would not, *he could not have spoken them*. His great knowledge of spiritual truths and his deep acquaintance with spiritual laws would effectually prevent him from falling into any such erroneous teaching as has been incorporated into the words I have just given. Both the words and their interpretation are a pure fabrication.

The rite of baptism is an ancient one, and it was long in existence before the birth of Jesus. Like so many others of its kind, it was begotten of ignorance of spiritual truths.

An initiation ceremony may be harmless of itself— and it can be equally useless. It is the false trimmings and the embroideries that are woven into the original fabric which cause the damage.

The erroneous teaching that baptism is essential to the 'soul's salvation' is completely opposed to the truths of the spirit world. Such interpolations abound in the New Testament. It is a flagrantly dishonest method employed by the Church to keep its members under its ecclesiastical thumb. It is but another instrument of fear with which to frighten its flock. It is but another example of the claims put forth by Orthodoxy for its exclusiveness.

The Christian, it is alleged, is in a vastly superior spiritual position because he is baptised, or he has enormously greater spiritual prospects than one who is not baptised. Indeed, the prospects for the unbaptised are pretty poor when they shall eventually arrive in the spirit world. Certainly, there will be no 'heaven' for them. Or if there be *some* kind of heaven for them, there will be no mistake about it.

They will be in this other heaven because they are

unbaptised, and therefore are merely tolerated since they have managed to lead fairly good lives while upon earth.

Their unbaptised state, however, must be always with them, and it is then too late to rectify the matter. They will never be able to see God *face to face*. That is the great penalty for their omission. There are supposedly others, but that is the greatest. A few words, however indifferently spoken, a little water sprinkled upon a person, give him the right and privilege to see God! Was ever spiritual presumption carried to further lengths!

In ancient days, when there was a wider knowledge of psychic lore, the use of water was better understood. But there was no mystic rite involved in its employment. It was merely used to assist in the operation of psychic force because water is a powerful conductor of such force, and water supplies a natural channel. Water is also a powerful cleanser of the etheric body, and it can effectively disperse whatever unpleasant influences may have gathered around the spirit body of incarnate man.

Water is therefore a double cleanser. It will wash the physical body and at the same time help to move whatever may be unwanted upon the spirit body. But there is no mystic, holy rite attached this perfectly ordinary function of cleansing. Under no consideration will bathing in the water remove the blotches and blemishes which are to be seen upon the spirit body as a consequence of the kind of life its owner lives.

The first and early use of water in this way was later misunderstood, and so became an initiation ceremony upon the validity of which so much depended.

Water is a splendid channel for the operation of psychic force. It is for that reason that Jesus chose the proximity of it when he felt that the occasion called for an extra flow of power. And where could one find a better body of water than that of lake or sea, and where could one be better situated than to be *upon* that water?

It is chronicled in the gospels that Jesus himself was baptised. He could have submitted himself to such a ceremony without undergoing any harm. He was not imbibing any false teachings. But with his superior knowledge he knew just what psychic effect the water would have upon him—and he constantly used it for that purpose. Such incidents and occasions remain unrecorded in the New Testament, or to be more accurate, they have been expunged from it.

The baptism 'ceremony' of Jesus which is recounted in the Scriptures is only *one* among the many scores of other occasions when the similar 'rite' was performed. In other words, Jesus was 'baptised' almost every day of his short life on earth, for the simple reasons I have given you. But the Church has transformed this natural action into a ceremony to be applied once only to any individual, in the normal course of things.

I foresee that possible exception will be taken to what I have said. That I cannot help. I speak the truth. But that, it may be countered, is a mere statement. Just so, it is a mere statement—of truth, none the less. How can I bring proof to you? Corroboration, perhaps, but how to bring proof? To ask others to come who will make the same affirmations as myself will only shift the responsibility on to their shoulders, and so it could go on indefinitely, gathering greater numbers in the process, it is true, providing more corroboration, which as between the incarnate and concerning affairs of the earth, would have ready credence, but as concerning spirit world, *no!*

So I must simply repeat that I am telling the truth as millions upon millions of us in the spirit world know it. The veracity of my statements will ultimately be demonstrated to every soul whose eye I have caught, so that if you challenge me here and now, so to speak, I will reply however much you may disagree with what I am recounting to you, however much you may wish to retain your opinions and ideas or those of the Church to which you belong, such stand-point cannot alter one iota the *truths* of the spirit world. I cannot alter them to suit the teachings of hundreds of years of Orthodoxy.

Therefore, I say that what I am now telling is what you must expect to discover, without fail, when in due course you arrive in the spirit world yourself.

Vicarious Atonement

A whole chapter—indeed a whole volume—might be written upon the crudities of religion. To us in the spirit world there appears so much in the religions of the earth world that is really crude, and most of it is a survival of what the earth calls paganism.

Again, from the point of view of the spirit world, there is often very little to choose between the peculiar rites as practised by some native tribe and the equally peculiar rites as performed by some of the Orthodox religions of the more 'civilised' parts of the earth world. The crudely carved idol of the natives has as much real significance in it as the upholding of some fantastic Christian belief.

It is the custom of the white man upon earth to sneer in a superior way at his dark brother because he is religiously so far in advance of the latter; and the latter is but a heathen, after all, who must be converted to the true religion—as expounded by the representative of the particular 'true' faith sent out to perform the task. The Christian does not realise that much of his religion has been taken bodily from that of the 'heathen'. The Christian sets an extraordinarily bad example to his black brother in other ways than in the enormous contentions which exist between one religious sect and another.

The Church to which I belonged when I was upon earth possesses some of the most elaborate of rites. It is, in fact, a vast and well-ordered religious organisation, having no doubts whatever upon any question or problem concerning the 'salvation' of man. Every contingency that is likely to arise in the lives and habits and thoughts of its adherents has been fully covered by the Church's laws and 'commandments'. Its members are bound, even as I was, by those laws and 'commandments', and individual religious interpretation is condemned.

In contrast to all this there are numerous earthly religions that practise a severe austerity in their services, admitting into them nothing which is not of the plainest description and completely free from all 'taint' of ritualism. The number of such religions upon earth is large, each disagreeing with the others in their beliefs, and each claiming more or less to be the 'one, true Church'.

From time to time, the earth world witnesses attempts at what some sections of the Church call 'Christian Unity', where members of a number of religious denominations meet to discuss their various beliefs in the hope of finding some 'least common factor' upon which they can all be in full agreement, and so effect thereby some sort of unity. These essays at spiritual unity are doomed to failure, and they will always be doomed to failure for just so long as the Churches are founded upon fallacious doctrines.

Between the two great extremes, which I have just mentioned to you, of elaborate ritual on the one hand and severe simplicity upon the other, every imaginable sort of religion and religious practice, creed, and dogma is to be found. The vastly varying and differing sects which are spread throughout the earth world, each with its numerous followers. amount in the aggregate to some *hundreds* of separate religious sects, and all of them claiming to have been founded upon some one injunction or another that was reputed to have been given by Jesus himself, or upon some text or other to be found elsewhere in the New Testament.

Each of these religious bodies will positively claim to be a true Church—if not *the* true Church—on the strength of its scriptural foundation. And in each form of religion, the New Testament is hailed as the true, inspired Word of God. Out of the inspired Word of God, then, there has come all this religious turmoil, and controversy and contention!

One of the principal articles of belief among early generations of man upon earth was the belief in the absolute need of offering sacrifices to the gods. They were mostly blood sacrifices of either human beings or animals. The offering of blood, it was earnestly believed in those far off days, was the only oblation acceptable to the gods, and the only means of appeasing their wrath.

How this could have pleased, or conciliated, or helped the particular god was one of the 'mysteries' of religion. This primitive and barbaric belief of the essential need for blood sacrifices has passed in the Christian religion, where people are still being taught upon earth that God sacrificed His only son upon the cross for the salvation of mankind.

Could any belief be of a more terribly gross nature; could any belief be ever a greater travesty of the *very* nature and essence of the Great Father of heaven and earth? Could any belief be more barbaric and horrible?

Is it to be wondered at when folk say that they do not know how to *love* God as they are taught to do by their religious instructors, when they are told that God, the Father, demanded not only a blood sacrifice, but that the sacrificial victim should be *His only* son. Could this be a God of love?—is a question that would spring to the mind of any normally constituted person.

To essay an answer to such a question is to lead one

into a wilderness of theological complexities which have little relation to the truth. The maintenance of such a doctrine as that God demanded a blood sacrifice of his son is to impute the most horrible and diabolical qualities to the Father of the universe. This sacrifice, ecclesiastics will tell you, was necessary for the remission of the sins of the people on earth. God demanded it, it will be affirmed. That is pure paganism—and without a vestige of truth behind it.

We are each responsible for our own sins. We must pay the penalty ourselves for any transgressions of spiritual laws; no one can do that for us. Thus is true justice administered throughout the spirit world to all alike, impartially, infallibly, and exactly.

'Redemption' cannot be bought for us. But even if 'redemption' were to be bought—by some strange mutation of spiritual laws—it would be a worthless article, because there is no individual in the spirit world, or upon earth, who could for one instant of time substantiate the claim of being a 'redeemer'.

Even the most illustrious souls, who dwell far and away above us here in these realms of light, even they have no power to remove the burden which mortal man can lay upon himself by the life he has led upon earth. Man is his own 'redeemer'. He always has been, and he always will be.

We cannot shift on to other shoulders the weight which we must carry ourselves. But we shall have every assistance in lightening that burden, and the means to do so will be shown to us readily upon our merest wish. That is as far as any person can go.

The Father of Heaven asks for no appeasement; He requires none. Neither does he need placating by the offering of sacrifices, albeit they be bloodless sacrifices.

In the spirit world we do not ever think in terms of 'body and blood'. Orthodoxy exults in the terms, and will point to the famous gathering of Jesus and his friends so shortly before he passed into the spirit world. At this last meeting he is supposed to have said, when taking bread and wine into his hands, this *is my body ... this is my blood*. And asked his friends to repeat this same assembly in his commemoration. From this simple wish has sprung a wealth of dogma and doctrine and ritualistic practices. In the latter there is supposed to be re-enacted the sacrifice, in a bloodless manner, which Jesus made upon his death. Let us examine the subject from the point of view of the spirit world.

Orthodoxy lays enormous stress upon the 'body and blood' of Jesus. What spiritual significance do they bear? The answer is *none*. The physical body is the vehicle which the spirit body uses during its sojourn upon earth. The blood that streams through that body is one of its vital forces, but the spirit body, which is resident within it, animates the physical body.

The blood that runs through the veins of the physical body can be released in such quantities that the physical body can no longer receive the animation of the spirit body. When you pass into the spirit world, you have no further use for your physical body. It counts as nothing in your mind.

By comparison with the superlative excellence of your spirit body, the earthly body was just a ponderous, awkward, and very vulnerable structure. But it served its purpose. With our new body we do not think in terms of 'body' and 'blood'. We have both, but they are indestructible and cannot be harmed. A 'sacrifice' of 'body and blood', that is to say, a religious service wherein a piece of bread is held to be the body of Jesus, and a cup of wine to be his blood, becomes, in the eyes of us here in the spirit world, a revolting conception.

If it is felt that a commemorative gathering would be helpful, then there is no reason why some description of service should not be held. But any suggestion, any, thought even, of 'body and blood' should be ruthlessly expunged. Incidentally, such service has very little spiritual value—*if any at all.*

The spirit world is not concerned with ritualistic observances whether they embody strange doctrines or not. The theologian will claim that such services are necessary for man upon earth if he is to have the 'grace of God' upon him. That is rubbish.

God is not dependent upon some trumpery religious device in order to pour down upon man His force and power. The force and power of the Father of the universe are to be had upon the instant and in any place whatsoever. Such downpouring requires no religious apparatus, no special building, no formularies, no man-made conditions or qualifications.

It may be objected that I am condemning communal 'worship' as of no account in the spiritual scheme of things; that the services of the Church, in fact, are useless. I do not condemn corporate services in the Church, but I do affirm that the majority of them are spiritually worthless.

A church service, of which the vital or central part is based upon a false doctrine, is completely worthless spiritually. Again, the object of such service must be taken into consideration. If it is intended as an act of propitiation to the Father, it is valueless. The Father needs no acts of propitiation.

If the service is performed because it is alleged that God demands worship, then again it has no significance. God does not ever *demand* worship of any kind or description. If the service be held for the 'remission of the sins' of the congregation, then once more the service is of no avail.

The most magnificent service ever conducted in the largest and most ornate cathedral with the maximum of solemnity, pomp, and ritualistic display, and in the presence of a whole hierarchy, will not, in the smallest, minutest degree remove from a single 'sinner' one fraction of the burden which a mis-spent life has loaded upon the shoulders of the breaker of spiritual laws. No pleading. However eloquently delivered or prolonged, will achieve that object.

Those peculiar religious devices, known to the orthodox world as the sacraments, through which, it is held, the grace of God will descend upon man, are just man-made institutions whereby the people can be kept in proper subjugation. Mysteries are necessary in maintaining the Church's power and authority. It would never do for the people to know as much as their ministers of the Church.

By withholding as much as possible, their fear of God is increased, and with that well inculcated, the people will do just as they are told. The authority of the Church will be maintained and all will be well—so authority itself may think.

All is *not* well. All is very ill. Indeed, with the countless thousands who have been misled, misguided, and befooled by their supposed religious mentors, the Church has built up an elaborate system of observances and doctrines, most of which, it will be claimed, have their foundation in the New Testament because they were actually instituted by Jesus himself.

Dishonest or ignorant scribes have put into the mouth of Jesus sayings which we, in the spirit world, know positively he could never have uttered. Jesus is supposed to have spoken about his 'Church'. That is a falsity of the worst kind. On no occasion was Jesus interested in establishing any Church. He dealt solely with spiritual truths; he was at no time concerned with the creation and establishment of peculiar sacramental devices upon which man's salvation would have to depend.

He knew that no one, either on earth or in the spirit world, can take upon himself the character or functions of a 'redeemer' or a 'saviour' in the sense in which those two terms are known, meant, and understood by the Church and most of its followers. Jesus dealt only with spiritual truths, not with religious fancies and their ritualistic trimmings. He stated the truth, bare and unadorned; he made no claims for himself beyond the fact that he knew and spoke the truth upon all matters appertaining to man's spiritual purpose and destiny.

Of the full comprehensive truth that Jesus spoke during his brief, active life upon earth, scarcely the smallest fraction has been recorded; that is to say, recorded for posterity to read. Much more was originally written down, but it was deleted. It was far too simple in its content to please some minds, especially those who could not see the sense in allowing the people to know too much about themselves and their spiritual make-up and destiny.

There was so little to be made out of the truth as Jesus proclaimed it. There were no mysteries with which to hold folk in spiritual subjection, to bring them to heel with fear of terrible punishments to come if they disobeyed authority. Primarily, God must be a God of Fear. If love came into the picture, it was merely done to temper the fear somewhat. The great thing was to avoid the wrath of God, because when He was not filled with wrath, then one could look for a display of that love.

From a simple farewell meal, taken in company with a dozen friends, there has arisen a form of church service which bears not the slightest resemblance to what it is supposed to commemorate. Those few friends were asked not to forget Jesus after he was gone from their presence physically. They were asked to meet in some such fashion, and by exercising the psychic faculties which they possessed, they would be enabled to see him again and hold converse with him collectively, as it had become their custom so to do.

While each one could by his own powers perceive Jesus, it was the pleasantest form of communion when they should foregather. Jesus could then tell them something more of the great unseen world, the spirit world, of which he had become a permanent resident. Those followers were happy that their great friend was able to be with them, though the world outside was unaware of it. The dreadful tragedy of his end upon earth was quickly submerged by his actual presence among them.

Indeed, it is the natural thing, here in the spirit world, to find that the glories of the new life, it beauties, its illimitable prospect, and its joys, collectively help to banish from the mind whatever unpleasantness, disaster, tragedy, or horrors may have been attendant upon the actual transition.

The process of elimination, as we might call it, may take a short or long period, according to various factors or circumstances, among which must be reckoned the mentality of the person concerned. It is the shock of transition that makes itself felt most prominently and not necessarily the mode of transition.

Here is another important point which it is well to emphasise. The actual process of passing permanently into the spirit world through the death of the physical body is *precisely the same with every human being born upon earth*. Although the physical causes of transition may vary a thousandfold, the spiritual process is exactly the same in all cases. Jesus was no exception to this natural spiritual law.

There was therefore no resurrection 'upon the third day' as it is usually stated in the different creeds. Resurrection just does not take place. Whither would a person arise—and whence? If an individual, following his transition, finds it expedient to lapse into the refreshing and revitalising sleep that is such a common occurrence in these lands, then he will do so. He will eventually awake; it may be after many months have elapsed or merely after the passage of an hour or two of earthly time. But that awakening is just an ordinary function, and it is no more a 'resurrection' than is your awakening every morning in your earthly bed—and for the same reason. You have in both cases merely emerged from a natural sleep. We do not have a 'resurrection' here in the spirit world, at any time of our lives.

The transition of Jesus, as far as the spiritual process is concerned, was exactly in accordance with the law that governs all transitions. The process does not admit of any alteration or variation, any modification or exception. The 'death' of Jesus and his speedy return in his spirit body to his friends demonstrated, to them, in the simplest and most convincing way, what he had himself told them so often during his earthly life. He proved to them beyond a shadow of doubt that man survives the grave, that 'death' means death of the physical body only; that the spirit body and the personality which it harbours are indestructible and imperishable.

He proved to them that death does not end everything; that man lives on and on. He showed them that while man can utterly destroy the life that is in the physical body, and commit butchery upon that body, the soul of man cannot be touched in the same way. Man cannot lose his soul.

Jesus clearly demonstrated to his old friends whom he had left behind that not only was life continuous and uninterrupted by death, but that it was possible and pleasurable and commendable and profitable for dwellers in spirit lands to return to the earth to visit their friends there, to talk with them, to help them and advise them where necessary, to continue the pleasant intercourse which the transition had seemingly disrupted.

Jesus showed that it was right and proper for the one world to hold converse thus with the other. And he came right into the midst of his friends on earth and offered them the comfort of his actual presence. He practised exactly what he had formerly preached—*blessed are they that mourn, for they shall be comforted.*

Those companions of old did not, in their sadness, have to turn to dismal texts; they did not have to trust in some mysterious and inexplicable 'faith'. They were not thrown back upon 'hope'. They were not told it was the 'will of God'. Instead, Jesus came and stood in their presence as one of them, as he had done a thousand times before when he was incarnate. His visible tangible presence did what no quotations from ancient chronicles could do; it did what no abstruse theological disquisition could ever accomplish. It brought supreme comfort and joy to a dozen or more sad hearts.

Jesus was the great exemplar of communication between our two worlds, yours and mine. He showed that with proper development and under proper auspices it is indisputably *right* for the two worlds to hold a normal converse through the exercise of psychic faculties in a normal rational way.

Jesus, among others, pointed the way for all mankind to follow, but Orthodoxy will have none of it. Communication with the spirit world is devilish and damnable, and no good can come of it. The whole thing reeks of hell, and if it does not drive a person mad, he will merely escape that to roast in hell for all eternity. None but evil spirits come back to earth, and they do so for the purpose of dragging down to their own filthy level those who are foolish or misguided enough to 'dabble' in such pernicious practices. It is all necromancy; a calling-up of the dead. The good spirit will not come. If any claim to be a good spirit, it is a devil masquerading as an angel of light. What unutterable puerile nonsense! And what colossal ignorance!

There will be some—perhaps many—who will affirm that not only am I a devil, but that I am the very Prince of Darkness himself. Let them think so if it gives them any satisfaction. There are others, far, far greater than I am, who have been regarded as demons from the realms of darkness, so that therein I find myself in good company!

'Thy Kingdom Come'

A little earlier, when we were discussing the Lord's Prayer, I suggested that I might be able to throw some light upon the joint relationship of our two worlds, and which might be, if you choose so to regard it, considered as giving some substance to the words *Thy kingdom come.*

The theological idea that the request is supposed to embody, namely, that God's spiritual kingdom may come to be spread throughout the whole world, is as vague as most theological ideas usually are. In fact, Orthodoxy has no clear notion in its mind as to what this clause in the Lord's Prayer can really mean. It has a pious sound and a truly spiritual ring about it, and it can obviously do no harm to retain the words and repeat them.

The words have recurred to my mind a number of times since I first came to dwell in these lands many years ago. In the spirit world, the Father of the universe is regarded as the King of Kings. But things are very different here in the spirit world as compared with the earth. We are for ever seeing evidence of the Great Spirit of all. Indeed, in these realms, and in many, many others, it is impossible not to see such evidence. It lives with us, and we live with it. But such things are not evident to earthly minds. How, then, according to the terms of the Lord's Prayer, was that kingdom to be extended to earth?

Let us go back a little while in history. What is most

important is that the people of the earth world are totally unaware of the spirit world that is existing round about them. It is only the comparative few, whose psychic faculties have been developed, who have any perception of the great world that is unseen to other folk.

Now from the beginning of time upon earth it was never intended that our two worlds should be thus separated by any barrier. Primitive man, as the early inhabitants of the earth are called, was not shut off from his brother in the spirit world in such a wholesale fashion as are you today.

Primitive though he may have been, primitive though he was in the eyes of today's earth world, yet his psychic talents were more highly developed generally, and were not confined to a relative few, here and there. The exercise of such powers was widespread. Yet man of those times is considered barbaric and uncivilised, and, from a religious point of view, nothing but a heathen!

The process of civilising the earth has had the effect of reducing in enormous proportions the possession of any psychic faculties at all. Thus, our two worlds have become more widely separated until those who possess any psychic powers are in the minority. They are the exception and not the rule. Man has paid the penalty for thus casting aside what he was meant to have and to use as his natural right upon earth, namely the power and ability to exercise those extra senses with which the spirit world could communicate with him.

It is authority in various forms that again is to blame for it was authority that gradually suppressed these powers in the people and retained them exclusively for themselves. But that exclusiveness brought with it its own penalty. Authority was denied communion with the spirit world by the spirit people themselves because it had no right to retain such powers in its own hands, for its own use and benefit, to the exclusion of all others. It was being used by authority for the furtherance of its own ends, and those ends did not coincide with the purposes of the spirit world. Mediumship, as the possession of psychic powers is named, was not totally destroyed, but it was limited to the few, and the world has suffered for it ever since.

The earth has become more civilised, so it is generally claimed, but has it? Science has advanced by gigantic strides since those early days, since the days, in fact, of Jesus himself. His times are not to be compared with the present day. Every sphere of life upon earth has marched forward, whether it be science, or art, or medicine, to name but three.

The earth, it would be claimed, is a gentler, nobler place since Jesus lived upon it. One has only to cast one's eyes about to observe patent signs upon every hand of the immense advances that have been made in all sections of society, and life upon earth has assumed a degree of comfort and pleasantness in normal times that was not only unthought of two thousand years ago, but unimaginable. But there is a flaw in this statement of the world's progress, and the very language in which we are now writing affords the most lamentable sign of just how far the earth has evolved spiritually.

There are two terms which have become of commonplace usage, and those terms are *war-time* and *peace-time*. For so long has life on earth been an alternation of peace and war that common terms are used to describe it. The words *war-time* and *peace-time* are as much part of the earth dweller's life, as are the words denoting the alternating seasons of *summer-time* and *winter-time*. That is a terrible indictment upon the people of earth.

What has all this, you will perhaps say, to do with

the kingdom of God? Precisely—what *has* it to do with the kingdom of God? The answer: it has nothing to do with the kingdom of God because any suggestion of that kingdom being established upon earth is frustrated, suffocated, nullified by the state of things that is existing upon earth at this present time, and that has been existing for hundreds of years. Great material progress has been made, but spiritual progress lags far behind.

Mankind is endowed with free will, and he has exercised that free will through the centuries, casting aside the great help which is ever at his call from the spirit world. The path was carefully chosen upon which man could walk to his advantage, but he chose to exercise his free will, and he did so to his own disadvantage.

The mere demanding of our rights does not necessarily mean that the awarding of those rights will eventuate to our advantage. The wise man will not insist in such cases, but prefer to listen to abler counsels. The earth chose to go its own way, and it has done so. It has effectively shut out the spirit world from all its governments and councils.

The Church has gone its own ineffective, futile way, powerless to prevent evil things from happening, and guilty itself of a long and ghastly catalogue of unspeakable horrors now known to the world as religious persecution, where so-called heretics were put to all manner of tortures because they tried to think for themselves, and where death was the order of the day for the enemies of the Church.

How can the Church lead a single soul when the Church itself is blind? It has been blind for centuries. It has no solution to the major problems which are confronting, and will continue to confront, the earth world for just so long as it continues to spurn the spirit world, and while people disbelieve in its existence, and, therefore, in the existence of its inhabitants. Or if, as church-goers, they believe in some sort of vague 'hereafter', that 'hereafter' has no concern with the earthly material present, and it can provide no solution to any problem whatsoever. It is the clever brains of the earth world who will find a way out of the morass. That remains to be seen, and seen it will be.

How can the kingdom of God come within a thousand thousand leagues of being established upon earth when the very people who talk about it so much and so loudly—the churchmen—have not the remotest notion of how to set about it? The delivery of eloquent addresses interlaced with the most lofty thoughts culled from the Scriptures will effect nothing.

The whole truth is that the earth cannot exist without the intervention of the spirit world, and that means it cannot exist without the direct assistance and advice of the great and wise ones of these spirit lands. Man could be inspired to perform gigantic deeds for the betterment of the whole earth, but he shuts himself off from almost every source of inspiration—except the lowest.

Inspiration does still take place, but its powers are circumscribed and its advantages limited by man's ignorance of the truth. As for direct communication with the spirit world, that is out of the question. The relative few who know of and practise communication with us—and they are few by comparison with the earth's populations—are not openly to be found among those who have the ordering of a country's affairs. Indeed, in some enlightened places people who hold converse with us are outlawed.

There are many tremendous problems which will come up in turn for solution, and solved they must be if the earth world is to survive. Man will doubtless endeavour to solve those problems for himself, thinking that he is a superior being with a superior brain. He will provide a great and impressive showing, and he will utter a voluminous number of words. The religious-minded people, as well as official religion, will sternly aver that unless the nations ask for God's help and guidance nothing can be achieved, and having asked for that help and guidance, they will provide no means for God to give them through his messengers of the spirit world.

There is no mistake about it, let me assure you. All the problems of the earth could be satisfactorily solved if the people of the earth would only turn to the people of the spirit world. In the spirit world there resides the purest wisdom, and from the immense reservoirs of this wisdom man is free to draw for whatever he may need.

If the people of the earth were to turn to the spirit world and the immeasurably wise beings who live here in the exalted realms. and in all earnestness were to place their social and international problems before them, they could, and they would, receive the precise plan and details for the enucleation of every problem, however complex it might be, that confronts the governments and nations of the earth. But those high beings would make one stipulation if success were to follow, and that is that implicit obedience to their directions would have to be accorded because by that means only would success be accomplished.

Of what good is it to pray *Thy kingdom come,* when not only do the incarnate make no attempt to bring it about, but, indeed, have not the remotest notion of *how* to bring it about? Merely praying for the kingdom of God will not suffice; something must be done by man himself to bring it to pass. And that will not be done by increasing the congregations in the churches; it will not be done by studying the Scriptures more assiduously.

It will not be done by a thousand 'calls to religion', whether those calls are made by self-appointed evangelists or by the whole of the hierarchy of the Church.

My friends may perhaps argue with me that if one were to follow the teachings of Jesus strictly, the world's difficulties would soon be settled, and a Utopian earth would be the result. Such an issue might be the case if *all* the teachings that Jesus gave had been fully recorded in all their exactitude. But they were not so recorded, and those that have been set down have a great many errors in them, the result of later tampering.

How far are the extant teachings of Jesus really observed by folk upon earth? Not very far, that is clear to see. But there are many and pressing questions that cry—and will cry—for solution, and which cannot receive any answer from the words of Jesus. The teachings of Jesus are spiritual teachings. The difficulties of the earth are in so many cases purely material and mundane. They cannot be regarded in the light of scriptural texts, and spiritual teachings will not offer a solution.

It is the concrete that is wanted, and the concrete is at the disposal of the people of earth if they will but approach the spirit world and ask for it.

Some of my good friends upon earth will perhaps laugh at me. They will say that my enthusiasm is running away with me; or that I am too much of a visionary; and that my suggestions are beyond all hope of accomplishment.

Then let me answer that I am not a visionary, and that my suggestions are *not* beyond all hope of accomplishment. In the first place, they are not mine *alone*. And they are based upon a common knowledge in these realms of terrestrial affairs generally.

We do not pretend to prophesying, but there are many things in these lands of which all its inhabitants are cognisant, but of which the earth world must remain in ignorance, though it is the fault of the earth that they should so remain in ignorance.

The gradual drift that has taken place on earth in man's affairs is a drift from spiritual truth and not *towards* it. The troubles of the earth have been brought upon man by his ignorance and folly, not by his supposed 'sinfulness', as some claim. If the drift persists, he will land himself in inextricable difficulties of such magnitude as the earth has never yet known.

Man upon earth is the most stubborn of creatures. He prides himself upon his common sense which, truly, he may possess in abundance. But a time comes when sense that is something better than merely common is urgently needed. Special sense is required, and that special sense, that wisdom, is not to be found upon earth. But it is to be found in illimitable abundance in the spirit world.

Now what I have just sketched to you can be regarded as something of a preliminary to the establishment of the kingdom of God on earth. It is that state in a modified form. There is a greater and fuller, indeed, more comprehensive sense, in which that state can be widespread over the earth. That brings us to the exercise of one's psychic faculties.

It is the custom on earth for many, many people not only to decry such abilities as are possessed by psychically trained persons, but is also the custom to deny the very existence of such faculties. There is only one description for such folk, and we do not hesitate to use it in the spirit world—they are *fools*. These realms are full of people who once, when they were on earth, denied that such things as psychic faculties existed. They know better now. They know that such faculties are part of the natural make-up of man.

They are not some strange idiosyncrasy displayed by peculiar people; something that is a little weird and uncanny, and rather unpleasant; something that is a trifle unhealthy and morbid; something that is, above all things, better left alone.

Science may, of course, put the matter to some laboratory tests, but that is different. Scientists can easily protect themselves. And if a scientist proclaims upon superficial examination that there is no evidence that psychic faculties exist, and less than no evidence that a spirit world and spirit people exist, then it will be just what was expected.

If, however, a scientist, more enlightened than his brothers in science, should proclaim that psychic faculties displayed through the mediumship of ordinary normal people *are* a reality, that the spirit world and spirit people *do* exist; and if he similarly announces that he has had superabundant and irrefragable evidence from his own relatives and friends in the spirit world, establishing their exact identity and the reality of the spirit world, then after such testimony there can only be one response; the scientist in question is in his dotage.

He may have been vastly clever in his own legitimate work, but he has at last reached his dotage, and is therefore not responsible for his freakish ideas about a 'hereafter'. He is enormously learned upon all subjects but this one, and upon this he is unreliable and must not be heeded. But psychic faculties and powers *do* exist, and there are thousands of folk who possess them and employ them for the good of their fellows.

All people possess the powers of mediumship inherently. In the majority of folk they want developing and bringing out, and regulating along adequate lines so that the best may be made of them, just as the artist and musician, shall we say, must develop his abilities by working upon the right lines. There is nothing unhealthy or morbid in such things because they are natural to man. It was intended that they should be so from the beginning.

Man upon earth was never meant to be cut off from the spirit world, neither was the spirit world meant to be cut off from intercourse with the people still upon earth.

Mediumship is the natural channel for communication, and by putting its powers into use man is fulfilling his proper destiny, not proceeding against his destiny, as he does by ignoring his own natural powers.

Now if the whole earth world were to become psychically developed in every branch of its exposition, the earth-plane would soon become a very different place. First of all, think of the universal sorrowing that would vanish from the face of the earth. When your friends pass at 'death' into the spirit world, those at the bedside would be able to see them depart in the capable hands of folk who had come to fetch them to their spirit home. You would be able to see them off, just as you do now when they go away upon an earthly visit.

Shortly after their transition, they would return to you filled with the buoyancy of the new life, excited with the glories they are enjoying as their right, and so ready to impart knowledge and give help to those still upon earth. Your friends would be seen coming into your rooms as naturally as though they were still incarnate, coming into your rooms as *they do now,* but, alas, to their sorrow, they are unseen.

They cannot give you that word of greeting, of help, of good counsel because they lack the means of getting it to you, directly or indirectly, even if, in the latter case, you would believe them were they successful. Your friends and relations would be ever willing to join in your many activities, ready to support you in your difficulties with their greater and wider knowledge, and with the still greater and wider knowledge upon which they can draw from wise and experienced beings from the higher realms.

They would not live your life for you. That would not be right, but by their co-operation they would—and could—make life upon earth nothing but the happiest, a fitting prelude to the wondrous happiness that is to be found here in these realms. So much sorrow and sadness, so much misery, would be eradicated, so much suffering, so many horrors and injustices, so many wrongs, would be removed from the earth if the two worlds could be thus joined together in unity of thought, word, and deed.

A unity of thought, word, and deed, as between the earth world and the spirit world. That is some approach to the realisation of the kingdom of God. Just think what it would mean to the populations of the earth. Freedom from fear, from fear of material unrest and difficulties, and the many insecurities that earthly life brings with it through the action of man in relation to his incarnate brother; and freedom from fear of what is to become of him when his earthly life ends.

Can the Church give man that freedom? The Church is incapable of it. All that the Church can do is to call for 'faith' upon the part of men, to put their trust in the mercy of God, to beg that Jesus may plead for them on that 'last dread day'.

The last dread day, indeed! What wicked teachings are these, when the truth is to be had for the asking? Is it to be wondered at that man is fearful for himself and his family and friends when he comes to think of the 'life beyond the grave'? Fear is dominating the earth world, and fear is not a good companion to harbour in one's house.

It is in the power of the spirit world to banish fear

from the mind of every soul upon earth, if the earth will but take the trouble to seek enlightenment. How can the kingdom of God be established upon earth when man is himself, through the power of Orthodoxy, trying to close and tighten the existing barriers between the two worlds?

The relative few upon earth who are aware of our existence in the spirit world and who call upon us for our help, the help which we are so happy to give, the comparative few who communicate with us regularly, such people know from joyous experience the enormous difference which the truth of spiritual things can and does make in their daily lives on earth. They can see something of the purpose of their lives upon earth; they know of the beauties, the natural beauties, of the life that awaits them when their earthly journey is done.

They are not dominated by a fear of what will betide them when their dissolution takes place. They are not frightened by dogmatic and doctrinal bogies that have no existence in reality. They are not frightened of us from the spirit world. A person is not frightened of his own father and mother when they are both incarnate. Why should the same person be frightened of them when, in the exhilaration of their life and in the splendid reality of the spirit world, his own parents go back to earth and try to speak to him?

That is not right, a man will say. They have gone to their 'eternal rest', and it would not be proper to disturb them. Besides, the Church says they cannot come back, or *would* not come back if they could. It is only devils that come back, impersonate our own kindred, deceive us, and thus try to ruin us spiritually, so that we jeopardise our 'immortal souls'.

What arrant nonsense! Poor blind man upon earth. The Church has led him astray, widely astray. It prays hard for the setting up of the kingdom of God upon earth; it professes to know so much, in the presumption of its assumed authority, about spiritual matters, and is perfectly content to go on in the same fruitless manner, fondly imagining that large congregations are a splendid sign of man's 'returning to God', satisfied to go on preaching the same useless doctrines which have no relation whatever to the truth, providing no solution to any of the earth's difficulties, powerless to right any wrong, and in many cases thoroughly indifferent to, or condoning, many wrongs of divers sorts, completely ignorant of one little item of sound information concerning a man's condition after he has 'died'.

The Church professes to have the spiritual care of man in its hands—and knows next to *nothing* about the matter at all. And that great and illustrious soul, whom the earth knows as, Jesus, sees from his exalted estate the havoc that has been wrought in the simple, direct, forthright teachings, the proclamation of which ultimately cost him his earthly life. He sees himself elevated into that deific position which never, for a single fraction of a second, did he imagine would be his in the minds of the people of earth.

He knows that he tried so hard to show people how they could make the earth into a gloriously happy place, to show people how the power of the Greatest Mind could be brought to earth through His benign representatives of the spirit world. He tried so diligently to show that if man would but listen to the voices from the spirit world all would be right with the earth, and that there would ensue a regime of happiness and repose for all men upon earth, the regime of the Father of the universe Himself, spreading right from its great source to the uttermost bounds of the earth. And all this would be accomplished through God's 'angels of light', whom an ignorant section of the earth call *devils*. God sends his ministers to earth, and the Church, which claims for itself as belonging to God, calls them emissaries of Satan!

The Church has become stupefied by its own fantastic doctrines and beliefs. It has become inflated by its own self-importance. It has become hypnotised by its own apparent security. It has become absorbed in the details of dogma and doctrine, and the outward displays of showy ritual. It has poured money into bricks and mortar because it really believes that the House of God warrants a lavish expenditure in art and architecture.

That may be justified only when all else is fully provided for—the poor people, for instance; for with the Father the needy come always first. But man himself can fitly be his own House of God, for he can send his thoughts, his petitions, and the expression of his needs from the privacy of his mind in his own home with equal—and probably better—effect.

As we see things in their clear light in the spirit world, we regard the Church on earth—and by Church I mean all those religious bodies who nominate themselves Christian—we regard the Church upon earth not as a help to man in his spiritual progression, but as a downright and deliberate hindrance. The Church is blocking the way to the diffusion of spiritual truth and knowledge throughout the earth world. It is no help to man in his journey through his earthly life, though seemingly it may be.

You have only to see for yourself the state of lamentable ignorance in which so many thousands upon thousands of kind and honest folk arrive in these lands of the spirit world. Their minds are clouded with crude and primitive beliefs, the choice gems from the ecclesiastical casket of spiritual teachings. They find the gems are but the veriest paste—and worthless. While the owner of them thought himself passing rich in spiritual knowledge, he finds himself bankrupt.

Man upon earth is scarcely living. He imagines he is, but in reality he is not, he sees all the signs of a material world round and about him, and overlooks, or forgets, the immense world and its gigantic populations that are unseen, namely, the spirit world. The Church prays for the coming of the kingdom of God, and visualises that kingdom as being, of course, essentially a Christian kingdom, with itself as its head upon earth. But the spirit world has different ideas upon the subject.

Now it may be objected that there are many things that must be altered on earth, many wrong things that must be swept away, before such a halcyon state of existence can be the case, and that it is man's duty to right these things himself, and perhaps would right them, but that there are too many obstacles in the way, the principal obstacle being man himself. That is so, but the wisest brains upon earth are far, far outmatched by wiser brains in the spirit world.

The earth lacks the wisdom and the knowledge on the one hand, and it lacks spiritual progression and evolution upon the other. The knowledge and the wisdom it can obtain from the spirit world; the means of progression and evolution will be revealed from that knowledge. The heart of man must change before life upon earth can become the true state of happiness it was meant to be. The Church is incapable of working any such change simply because it has no knowledge of the spiritual truth.

It deals very glibly in heaven and hell, knowing nothing of the former, and threatening with the latter, and the general prospect held out for most people is a gloomy and depressing one.

If the psychic faculties of all men on earth were fully developed, each according to his particular make-up, man would learn the truth at first hand. The truth would show him which way it were better to proceed for his soul's welfare. He would learn of the consequences of evil ways; he would learn also of the beauties that a life of service to his brother will bring him. Life upon earth would be lived by all folk according to the perfect laws of the spirit world, and not according to the many discriminating laws and modes of living as at present upon earth.

Moral justice would go hand in hand with legal justice, and the supreme guidance of wise beings in the spirit world would ever be at the disposal of earth folk in the solution of any and every difficulty. Those of the incarnate who are in direct communication with even the humblest of us here know just what the help of the spirit world means in their daily lives. We can help to smooth the way through life for them to the utmost of our abilities and what can thus be done individually can also be done nationally and internationally.

In the kingdom of God on earth, no person would be overlooked, neglected, or forgotten. The many injustices under which man labours now upon earth would be righted if those who are responsible trusted a little less to their own 'wisdom', and sought a little of the *real* wisdom of the spirit world. Man on earth has not so far made a very brilliant success of conducting the affairs of the earth. In truth, he is not yet capable of doing so, but he will not realise it.

The earth is faced with many acute difficulties. They are acute at present, but they will become chronic if they are not dealt with adequately and finally. Man is laying up a dreadful store of unhappiness in the future for the earth world if, in the very superior attitude of mind he adopts towards the spirit world, he tries to close the door upon us altogether. He will not succeed, of course. It was tried nigh upon two thousand years ago in a small corner of the earth.

Orthodoxy—of another sort, but equally bad—was responsible for the great tragedy of Calvary, and Jesus, who dealt only in spiritual *truth,* was the victim. It was not the Father of the universe who demanded the sacrifice of His only son to redeem the world. That is a monumental untruth. It was Orthodoxy that would not listen to the truth that caused the transition of Jesus. And Christian Orthodoxy has done no better. It has opposed the very truth that Jesus himself came to give to humanity. It opposes the truth at this exact moment of time. But—*magna est veritas, et praevalebit.*[1]

The Church has assumed responsibility for the spiritual care of man upon earth, and the Church has failed dismally. It is in most respects an impostor, for in professing to know much, it knows very little which can be of spiritual service to man. It can provide no answers to vital questions, questions that are in the minds of so many people. Can the Church answer these questions, for instance, as applied to yourself: What becomes of me when I die? What has become of all my relatives and friends? Why is there this seemingly profound silence between them and me?

To the last question I would answer such folk that there is no need, no need whatever, for that profound silence, for it can be and is broken, just as I have broken it, even as I am now breaking it to you, my good friend, and even as I shall continue to break it for just so long as I can serve a good and wholesome purpose.

Man on earth should have no fear for his spiritual future. He should be able to live his good life upon earth in complete happiness of mind, and in complete freedom from fear for his future in the spirit world.

We are not devils, though there are plenty of evil

---

1. Truth is mighty and will prevail.

people in the spirit world, but it is not the spirit world that has made them evil. It is the earth world that has sent them here in that state. The clergy of the Church, or some of them, consider us as devils.

There are clergymen still upon earth who fully qualify for that designation themselves, but that is not to say that all ministers of religion are devils. The same stupid cry of devils was put up in the time of Jesus and in the same connection. Let people forget the devils and think of other folk in the spirit world who are eager and waiting to speak to them.

Now, my good friend, these present writings must close. We have touched upon a great theme only in a very abbreviated fashion, but then the subject is itself enormous. So, I have felt that it would be best to treat of a few matters from the New Testament, rather than to take a broad survey of the whole, which would perforce remain sketchy. There is much, so very much, that I have left unsaid and which we have not even considered remotely, but I shall hope to speak to you again upon kindred matters and go into other questions which I am obliged here to omit.

But in the little that I have said, it is my earnest hope that I have shed some light, and perhaps pointed the way for my friends to study a great book—the New Testament—with their critical faculties fully alert, and not to be misguided by unreliable traditional interpretations of what are perfectly plain statements of the truth, and not to be misled by others who, in assuming the role of spiritual teachers, are not in a position to give the truth, although they are in the position to *learn* the truth from the spirit world—had they the wit to do so.

I do not profess to be your spiritual teacher. That would be presumption upon my part, but I can give you some of the knowledge—the common knowledge of these Realms—which I have gained since I left the earth world for the greater and more beautiful spirit world.

Here, so much has been made plain to me. I am anxious to pass on that news to you that your life on earth may be made that much happier, and your understanding that much clearer. It is a little thing to do for so much that I have received. My debt has increased since I first began to speak to my friends upon earth, for it is from those same good friends, whose encouraging thoughts have always reached me, that so much unreserved kindness has been shown to me in the attention which my words have been accorded.

Benedicat te omnipotens Deus.

[Almighty God bless you.]

www.ingramcontent.com/pod-product-compliance
Lightning Source LLC
LaVergne TN
LVHW051126080426
835510LV00018B/2246